Marie-Louise and the Invasion of 1814

Maria Luigia

Marie-Louise and the Invasion of 1814

The Empress and the fall of the First Empire

Imbert de Saint-Amand

LEONAUR

Marie-Louise and the Invasion of 1814;
The Empress and the fall of the First Empire
by Imbert de Saint-Amand

First published under the title
Marie-Louise and the Invasion of 1814

Leonaur is an imprint
of Oakpast Ltd

ISBN: 978-1-84677-950-3 (hardcover)
ISBN: 978-1-84677-949-7 (softcover)

http://www.leonaur.com

Contents

1

The Opening of the Campaign

The description of Paris and of the army during the invasion is gloomy and painful reading. The Parisians, with few exceptions, manifested no heroism. In spite of the urgent danger, all the theatres remained open. The capital, with its usual frivolity, showed none of the deep feeling which promises obstinate resistance. The prevailing impression was one of weariness with war. Treason was everywhere latent, obviously awaiting only a good opportunity for breaking out. The National Guard refused to march outside of the city. The officials took more thought of themselves than of their country.

Whether Napoleon or the foreigners should be applauded depended only on the chances of war. Paris, alternating between groundless hopes and the blackest despair, never faced the situation fairly. All those that had been expelled by the police returned in the general confusion, asserting that they would have been deemed criminal if they had remained in the departments occupied by the enemy. People came from a distance of more than thirty leagues to find safety for their family and their belongings in the capital. The farmers of the neighbourhood drove in their herds and flocks to the suburbs. The population suddenly increased enormously, and space was lacking for the new arrivals.

The most disturbing rumours were everywhere current, spreading gloom and discouragement. In drawing-rooms, in shops, in the streets, there was endless discussion of the impending catastrophe. As was said by the Duke of Rovigo, at that time Minister of Police, coercion would have hastened a revolution, and the slightest consolation that could be given to the suffering multitude was to leave it free to indulge in lamentations; there was no lack of grounds for numerous arrests, but, in justice, the prisons would have had to be doubled, to hold all those more or less deserving of incarceration.

The army, inspired by a patriotism more fervent than that of the Parisians, did its duty and more than its duty. It fought and suffered with a heroism worthy of a better fate. It is hard to say which were the more admirable, the beardless youths or the gray-haired veterans. Men like them would have saved France, if France could have been saved; but, in spite of their tireless energy, their indomitable courage, they felt that they were doomed by fate. Napoleon, with all his genius, knew no more of those lucky, almost miraculous chances which had so often saved him from apparently certain ruin at the beginning of his career. The setting of the sun bore no likeness to its rising, and soon there was to fall the night in which the Imperial star was extinct.

Nevertheless, the opening of the campaign showed no lack of brilliancy. Napoleon, who had left Paris, in the morning of January 25, 1814, reached Châlons-sur-Marne the same day. His generals said he must have brought troops with him. "No," he answered coolly; and then when they were in consternation at this confession he filled them with new hope by his bold plans.

"No one is ever beaten unless by his own consent. Doubtless we shall have dark days, when we shall have but one man against three, or even four; but we used to do that when we were young, and we ought to know how to do it now that we are old. . . . We have won every form of glory; we must win the last which is the crown of all; that is, to face bad luck and triumph over it."

The next day, Wednesday, January 26, at noon, Empress Marie Louise, surrounded by the princes of the Imperial family, the high dignitaries, the Ministers, the high officers, the Grand Eagles of the Legion of Honour, the ladies and officers in waiting, received, in the Throne Room at the Tuileries, a deputation of the National Guard of Paris.

Marshal Moncey, Duke of Conegliano, presented her with an address: "Madame," he said, "His Majesty the Emperor and King has deigned to permit his faithful subjects, the officers of the National Guard of Paris, to lay before the throne the expression of their love and fidelity. These they have endeavoured to express in this way: Sire, on his departure to assume command of the armies, Your Majesty confides his beloved wife, his son, the nation's hope, and entrusts the security, the tranquillity of the capital, to our love, our fidelity, our courage. Your noble words, Sire, have found an echo in our hearts.

Would that they had been heard as well in the remotest corners of France! Depart, Sire, with confidence. Let no disquiet about the fate of what you and we hold most dear, trouble your great thoughts. Go with our sons and brothers to drive away the assembled forces of the enemy ravaging our provinces. To the strength of your troops and to the power of your genius, we shall add the power of public spirit, aroused by our country's danger, by the might of national pride, indignant at the insolent pride of the foreigners, and very soon the enemy will recognize the imprudence of their undertaking and the falsity of their hopes. . . . On receiving the crown, Sire, you received also our oaths. We lay them once more before Your Majesty, before your revered wife, so worthy of your love and of ours. Before the cradle of your august son, Madame, we beg Your Majesty to convey the expression of our feelings to your august spouse."

They were hastening to burn what was left of the Imperial incense; soon they were to be offering it before the Royalists.

January 27, at eight in the morning, Napoleon entered Saint Dizier. On seeing him, the despondent populace took new courage and became more hopeful. A letter from this place, dated January 28, was printed in the *Moniteur*. It ran thus:

> The enemy were here two days ago, committing deeds of violence, respecting neither age nor sex. Women and old men were exposed to their insults and maltreatment. The arrival yesterday of the French troops put an end to our

sufferings. The Emperor's entry was the occasion of most touching scenes. The whole populace gathered about him; all our sufferings were forgotten. An old colonel, M. Bouland, who is seventy years of age, threw himself at his feet which he bedewed with tears of joy, and gave expression both to all the grief that a brave soldier must feel at seeing his native land polluted by the presence of the enemy, and his joy at seeing them in flight before the Imperial eagles.

Napoleon, with all the ardour of his youth, manoeuvred to prevent the junction of the army of Silesia, commanded by Blücher, with that of Bohemia, commanded by Schwarzenberg. For the conflict he had but fifty thousand men to oppose to the two hundred and thirty thousand of the enemy; nevertheless he was full of confidence. His plan was to throw himself on the flank of the forces of the Coalition, to surprise them by this attack, which should disconcert and possibly destroy the enemy. That is why he left the Marne, turning suddenly to the right, towards the Aube. His aim was Brienne, which Blücher was passing through at that moment. He made his way through the dark forest by a straight road which favoured his impatience. At Maizières, a village near Brienne, he said to the National Guards, who were crowding about him:

> We fight today for our firesides, and must defend them well, and not let the Cossacks get to them. They are wretched guests, and will not leave any room for you. Let us show them that every Frenchman is born a soldier, and a good soldier.

The Emperor recognized the *curé* of Maizières as one of his former regents of the College of Brienne. "What! It's you, my dear master!" he exclaimed. "So you have never left the country? So much the better! You will be all the more competent to serve the nation. I needn't ask if you know the neighbourhood."

"Sire, I could find my way everywhere blindfolded."

"Then come with us; you will be our guide, and we can talk."

The old *curé* mounted the horse of Roustan the Mameluke and became the guide of the army.

January 29, was fought the battle of Brienne, between Napoleon and Blücher. The town, divided into four sections by two intersecting streets, was lost and taken several times. One moment the Emperor thought that Blücher had been made prisoner. "We've got the old swordsman!" he shouted; "the campaign will be a short one." But he was mistaken; the Prussian general had not been captured; he was retreating. The French conscripts, though the enemy was two to one, finally defeated the veterans of the Coalition.

January 31, 1814, Napoleon wrote from Brienne to his brother Joseph:

> The affair at Brienne was very hot. I lost three thousand men, and the enemy four or five thousand. I pursued the enemy half-way to Bar-sur-Aube. I had the bridges over the Aube, which had been burned, repaired. A minute more and General Blücher with his whole staff would have been captured. The nephew of Chancellor von Hardenberg was captured by their side; they were on foot and did not know that I was with the army. Since this fight, our troops have a high reputation with the Allies, who had doubted of their existence. This battle, the position of our armies, and their reputation, may hasten a peace. It would be well for the Paris newspapers to speak of the preparations for defence and of the arrival of many troops from all quarters.

After the battle, Napoleon established his headquarters in the castle of Brienne, where he spent two nights.

> "During this stay," says Constant, his *valet de chambre*, "I recalled that of ten years earlier at this same castle, when he was on his way to Milan to add the title of King of Italy to that of Emperor of the French. Now, I said to myself, not only is Italy lost to him, but in the middle of the French Empire, only a few leagues from his capital, the Emperor is defending himself from numberless enemies.

Most of those with him, accustomed to count on his good fortune, still trusted to it; yet we could not deny that there had been a great change. It was very plain that we were in front of a mass of foreigners whom hitherto we had seen only in their own countries, and who now were in our country in their turn."

General de Ségur also describes Napoleon returning after so many distant victories to the military school of Brienne, where he had spent his youth, and finding it ravaged, filled with corpses, littered with ruins. Then the battle-worn soldier was moved. He meditated on the many evils of which he was the main cause, and yearned to repair them. To console the inhabitants for their losses he lavished money out of his own purse. Hearing that many young and beautiful women had in their terror sought refuge in the cellars of the castle, he had them brought out, and consoled them himself, inviting them to dine at his own table. He told them that he would rebuild the town, that he would buy the castle and turn it into a fine military establishment, or, rather, into an Imperial palace. After dinner, memories of his boyhood recurred to him, and he talked for some time, ending with this melancholy exclamation:

Could I have imagined then that I should have to defend this town against the Russians!

At Brienne, in the severe winter of 1783, he had made bastions, parapets, and trenches in the snow, and divided the pupils into two camps. He made himself commander-in-chief of the besieging forces and led them to the attack with such vigour that the game had to be stopped, many of the contestants having received real wounds. Alas! How many other men was he to have killed or wounded in his terrible career! When he recalled the winter of 1783, did he think of the winter of 1812?

"When we were at Malmaison," says Bourrienne, "how often, when we were walking in the path leading to the plain of Rueil, did the village bell interrupt our most serious conversations? Bonaparte used to stop in order not to lose any of the sound, in which he delighted. It used to impress him so strongly that he would say to me, with emotion:'That recalls my first years at Brienne. Then I was happy!' When the sound was silent, he would resume his vast reveries."

Yes, then he was happy! But when his dreams had come true, when he had attained an immense, unrivalled glory, and torrents of blood had been shed, what did it avail him? The plain uniform of the pupil was better than coronation robes; the innocence of childhood better than the conqueror's pride! His thoughts must have been bitter; his remorse, keen.

But the noise of battle soon interrupted Napoleon's reveries. From the hill of Brienne he looked down on the plain of Rothière, where, January 31, the two armies confronted each other. The battle was to be fought the next day, with all the chances against the thirty-seven thousand Frenchmen, who had to contend with one hundred and fifty thousand of the enemy. The sky was dark; the snow was falling heavily. January was going out in gloom, and the month of February was to be even more terrible. It was with a certain satisfaction that Paris had heard of the success at Brienne, but optimism was not common.

The disasters had been too frequent for any confidence to be felt in Napoleon's star. The newspapers in the pay of the government in vain sought to arouse confidence; confidence did not come at command. The same distress filled the Emperor's headquarters and the Tuileries. Even Marie Louise, in spite of the atmosphere of flattery in which she lived, in spite of the pains taken to conceal or to lessen every painful truth, was anxious and alarmed. Chamberlains, ministers, officials, try as they might, could not wear the confident look of earlier days. All these frightened courtiers resembled a band of stray actors who do not know whether the theatre they are playing in one evening will admit them the next.

2

The First Fortnight of February

No drama is more crowded with incident and anguish than is the campaign of 1814, a bitter struggle between despair and hope, between the force of events and genius. Neither Champaubert nor Montmirail, those days of miracles, were to save the Empire; yet what glory there was in the disasters of this fatal and memorable war! Meissonier, the artist who has at times done such great painting on minute canvases, has reproduced better than anyone the sombre and austere poetry of this unhappy period. His Napoleon on horseback, sad and solemn, in a colourless plain half covered with snow, is advancing slowly, as if clogged by fate.

His generals are following him in silence; their sturdy but sad faces show that only their heroism preserves them from discouragement. All the sufferings and all the deceptions of France violated, invaded, mutilated, seem to be united in this picture, which inspires a feeling of patriotic pity. The conqueror's faults are forgotten, his contempt for human life, his grand but futile plans, his haughtiness, only equalled by his genius; the despot yields to the soldier; we pity his anguish because it is not that of a common man, even of a monarch, but that of an entire nation.

The separation of some of the provinces from France was like maiming the Emperor himself. Madame de Staël, his implacable foe, said:

Bonaparte's campaign against the Allies, in the winter of

1814, is generally recognized as very fine, and even the Frenchmen whom he had proscribed could not keep from wishing that he might succeed in saving the independence of their country.

It was a vigorous and obstinate defence that he made, one directed by a sure hand. In his wrath with fickle fortune, Napoleon fought with indignation and rage.

The insulting propositions of European diplomacy aroused his wrath to such a degree of fury that his energy became more than human in his struggle, not merely against fate, but against remorse, against his conscience, which reproached him bitterly for having gone to Moscow to arouse the Cossacks and to tempt them to the banks of the Seine. In his petty army, tried by sublime devotion and courage, were heroes, some with smooth faces, others with gray beards; there were young men with the same fervour as the young men of 1792, veterans whom misfortune, after so much glory, found firm and indomitable. As Lacordaire said in his funeral oration over General Drouot: "The hour for great souls is that when everything is lost!"

February opened disastrously; on the first day of the month Napoleon lost the battle of Rothière: thirty-seven thousand men could not triumph over one hundred and fifty thousand. Though defeated, the great general remained impassable amid a storm of bullets and cannon-balls, saying to those who urged his withdrawal to a place of safety, "No; leave me alone: don't you know that our days are numbered?"

In the night it was only with difficulty that he decided to beat a retreat. So great remained his ascendancy over his enemies that they did not pursue him; they could not believe in their own success, and when the sun rose in the morning of February 2, it was an hour before the sight of the vast empty plain convinced them of their victory.

February 3, King Joseph wrote to the Emperor: "Yesterday and the day before there was too much confidence; today there is too little. Today I have visited the outposts on the left bank; they will be in readiness in three days. I was much pleased with the aspect of the suburbs." And February 5: "Today I found much despondency, and I had great difficulty in encouraging a number of persons. I have seen the Empress twice, and I left her in a calmer state last evening; she had just received a letter from Your Majesty in which mention was made of the Congress. If Your Majesty should meet with serious reverses, what form of government should be left here to prevent conspirators from heading a movement? Jerome asks me what is to be done in this case. Men are coming, but we have no money for their equipment."

Every day swelled the general alarm. Napoleon wrote from Troyes, to Joseph, February 6:

Have everything valuable removed from Fontainebleau, and especially everything that might figure as a trophy, yet without stripping the palace.

The same day the Emperor, hearing that the invaders were outflanking him and moving towards Paris, perceived that he had to leave Troyes. Thirteen leagues of territory were abandoned by this retreat. The soldiers marched in utter gloom. "When are we to halt?" was the question on every one's lips.

The 7th they reached Nogent, where, for a few hours, everything seemed hopeless. Napoleon was distraught by the necessity of thinking of the capital, alive with Royalist intrigue; of the battlefields, where he was perpetually risking his own life and the future of France; of the Congress of Châtillon, where negotiations were going on while the armies were fighting, and whence came propositions, each more humiliating than the one before. It was hard for him to keep his head amid so many dangers. Bad news arrived from every quarter of the Empire, like birds of evil omen crowding to a single spot.

Two hundred and fifty thousand Frenchmen were scattered about most needlessly, —fifty thousand on the Elbe, one hundred thousand under the Pyrenees, and a hundred and fifty thousand beyond the Alps. What might not these two hundred and fifty thousand men have accomplished if they had not been scattered

in this useless way? There was still a chance for safety, if Murat could unite with Prince Eugene to attack the Austrian rear. But, to the general amazement, Murat had become the ally of the Austrians and the English.

Napoleon, betrayed on every side, wrote in utter sadness:

It is my marriage that has wrought my ruin! I don't complain of the Empress, but counted too much upon the Austrians! My father-in-law, Metternich, their army corps which served under my flag in 1812, have deceived me! And, finally, you see that everything, even the winter, has conspired against me. The earth, which was frozen hard on the eve of my march to Brienne, turned to mud the next day. Marmont remained there, and that unfortunate affair at Rothière, which I could not avoid, makes peace indispensable. My soldiers are unwilling to fight any more.

The Allies had invaded Aix-la-Chapelle, Liège, Brussels, all Belgium. They had again taken possession of the Marne, captured Vitry, and forced Châlons to surrender. As a condition of peace they insisted on confining France within its old boundaries, the boundaries of 1790.

"What!" exclaimed Napoleon; "ask me to sign such a treaty, to trample upon my oath! Unheard of reverses have forced me to renounce further conquests, but to abandon those of the Republic, to destroy what was confided to my keeping, and after so many efforts and so many victories, to leave France smaller than I found it, never! It would be treason and cowardice. You fear the prolonging of the war, and I fear still more certain dangers which you do not foresee! Consider! What should I be to the French after putting my signature to their humiliation? What answer could I make to the Republicans of the Senate when they came to ask of me once more the boundary of the Rhine?"

Nevertheless, the Emperor's counsellors, deeming longer resistance hopeless, besought him to yield. All night long Napoleon lay awake; his heart torn by anguish, and he was heard to mutter in a dull, broken voice: "Very well; yes, you shall have peace, you want it—but you will see that it is a disgraceful peace!"

At this time Paris was overwhelmed with terror. Joseph wrote to Napoleon, February 7:

The evacuation of Châlons has thrown us all into consternation." And Marie Louise wrote to Joseph the next day: "The Emperor tells me not to worry. You know that is impossible." Already people began to think of the possibility of the Empress's departure. February 7, at eleven in the evening, Joseph wrote to Napoleon a long letter from which we make this extract: "I am very desirous that the Empress shall not depart. We cannot hide from ourselves that the alarm and despair of the populace would have sad and fatal results. I think, as do all whose opinion I value, that we should make every sacrifice before proceeding to this extremity. Men devoted to Your Majesty's government fear lest the Empress's departure would drive the people of the capital to despair, and hand over the capital and the Empire to the Bourbons. While I thus give utterance to the terrors which I read on every face, Your Majesty may be assured that his orders will be executed by me with the utmost fidelity as soon as I receive them.

Napoleon received this letter at Nogent, at the very moment when he thought that nothing was left for him but to die on the field of battle. His letter in reply was published for the first time in full, by the Baron Ducasse, in his interesting volume, *The Royal Brothers of Napoleon I.* Here are a few passages from this letter, dated Nogent, February 8, 1814, 4 a.m., which was to have such disastrous consequences before the end of the following month:—

My Brother: I have received your letter of the 7th at 11 p.m. It surprises me much. I have read King Louis's letter, which is a mere rhapsody; that man has but little judgment, and he never grasps a question properly. I have spoken to you about the case of Paris, that you should not call the end in question anymore; it concerns more people than me. When that happens, I shall be no longer alive; consequently, I don't speak for myself. I told you, about the Empress and the King of Rome, what the circumstances indicate, and you have failed to understand what I said. You may be sure that if that contingency arrives, what I foretold to you will infallibly happen. I am sure that she too has a presentiment of this [an allusion to Marie Louise, who thought that the Emperor would get himself killed]. King Louis speaks of peace, which is giving his advice at a very improper time. Moreover, I don't understand your letter at all. I thought I had explained everything to you; you never remember anything, and you always agree with the first man who talks to you and impresses his views on you. I repeat it then: Paris will never be occupied while I am alive; I have the right to be believed by those who hear me.

Those who reproach General Ducrot for his celebrated proclamation at the siege of Paris should reflect on this broken promise. But to return to the letter of February 8, 1814:

Afterwards, if by force of circumstances which I cannot now foresee, if I should move towards the Loire, I should not leave the Empress and my son far from me, because, in any event, it might happen that they would be captured and carried to Vienna; and that would happen all the sooner if I were no longer alive.

Referring to Talleyrand, Fouché, and a few others, the Emperor went on:

I do not understand how, during these intrigues under your very eyes, you express such imprudent praise of the proposition of traitors unworthy of advising any honourable course. Yes, I will be frank with you; if Talleyrand shares this opinion about letting the Empress leave Paris, in case the enemy should approach, it is treason. I say to you once more, be on your guard against that man; that is what I have done for sixteen years. I have ever been kind to him; but he is certainly the greatest enemy of our house, now that fortune has for some time abandoned us. Regard the counsel I give you; I know more than those people.

If a battle should be lost, and news of my death should come, you would hear of it before anyone else. See that the Empress and the King of Rome leave at once for Rambouillet; give orders to the Senate, the Council of State, and all the troops to assemble on the Loire. Leave at Paris a prefect and an Imperial Commission or some of the mayors.

But do not let the Empress and the King of Rome fall into the enemy's hands. Be sure that from that moment Austria, being no longer interested, would carry her to Vienna with a generous allowance, and under the pretext of seeing the Empress happy, would force the French to adopt whatever the Regent of England and Russia might suggest. Every party would find itself thereby destroyed, while, in the opposite case, the national spirit of the great number of those interested in the revolt would render every result incalculable. It is to the interest of Paris that the Empress and the King of Rome do not stay there, because this interest cannot be divided from their persons, and because, since the foundation of the world, I have never known of a monarch's being captured in an unfortified town: it would be the first case.

In the confusion of a great crisis, one does what one has to do, and lets the rest go. Now, if I live, I am to be obeyed; and I have no doubt of this obedience. If I die, my son reigning and the Empress Regent ought, for the honour of the French, not to let themselves be taken, and should retreat to the remotest village. Remember what the wife of Philip V. said. Indeed, what would be said of the Empress? That she abandoned the throne of her son and of ourselves; and the Allies would prefer to end everything by carrying her a prisoner to Vienna. I am surprised that you don't see that. It is evident that every one's head in Paris is turned by fear.

This memorable letter ended with this fear, or, more truly, this prophecy:

For my part, I had rather my son should have his throat cut than that I should see him brought up in Vienna as an Austrian prince; and I have a high enough opinion of the Empress to be sure that she shares this opinion so far as a woman and a mother can.

Suddenly, just when everything seemed absolutely hopeless, after the night of February 8, in which there were prepared for the Duke of Vicenza, the French plenipotentiary at the Congress of Châtillon, despatches pacific even to humiliation, Napoleon learned that Blücher, with perilous audacity, had entered Brie, in Champagne, and was making forced marches on Paris. At once the Emperor, as if arousing from a disturbed sleep, breathed new hope, and resolved to make the Prussians pay well for their boldness by suddenly falling on their flank. With the eye of an eagle about to seize his prey, he saw the very point where he was to attack them.

Then passing in a moment from the blackest despair to boundless confidence, his pride reviving and filled with regret for the concessions he had prepared himself to make, he expected to regain everything by a single stroke. He saw himself already victorious over the Coalition, driving it over the frontiers, pursuing it beyond the Rhine, the Elba, the Vistula. Her was bending over his maps, measuring distances with a compass, when the Duke of Bassano entered the room with the despatches prepared in the night for the Congress.

"Oh! It's you!" exclaimed Napoleon. "Well, we have something very different before us now. I am now preparing to beat Blücher. He is advancing by the Montmirail road; I shall leave and beat him tomorrow and the next day. If this movement is as successful as it ought to be, the state of affairs will be entirely changed, and then we shall see."

Then followed a series of wonders, like the most brilliant days of the Italian campaign. The 10th, Napoleon beat the Russians at Champaubert; the 11th, he won the bloody victory of Montmirail over the Prussians; the 12th, he pursued the fleeing foe and triumphed at Château-Thierry; the 14th, he beat Blücher at Vauchamps. It had taken him only five days to disorganize the army of Silesia, and to capture twenty-eight thousand men of this army of sixty thousand. This brilliant result, this series of victories, made a great impression on Paris, without, however, seriously affecting the natural alarm of the populace. Yet Joseph, having heard of the victory of Champaubert, had written to Napoleon, February 11: —

Sire: I received Your Majesty's letter at the moment I was reviewing the National Guard of Paris in the courtyard of the Tuileries. I communicated the good news to the officers, who were filled with the utmost enthusiasm. Six thousand men of the National Guard were present, well equipped and in excellent spirits. The King of Rome was at his window, and was greeted with cries of 'Long live the Emperor!' I also told the news to the Councillors of State, and all Paris is joyous; for in fact the national honour is not extinct. The Empress, whom I saw before she went out, and whom I have just seen again, has ordered that cannon be fired, and that the news be announced at the theatres this evening.

The Imperial star still shone bright just before setting. Never had Napoleon shown himself a more skilful tactician. One short, heroic week had been enough for him to capture from the Allies five generals, sixty-eight cannons, many wagons and stores, and more than twenty-eight thousand prisoners. The army of Silesia which, on the 9th of February, had been only twelve leagues from Paris, was driven back by the 14th to forty leagues. Napoleon, desirous that the capital should still believe in its Emperor's genius and good fortune, gave orders that the eighteen thousand prisoners he had captured at Champaubert, Montmirail, Château-Thierry, and Vauchamps, should be at once despatched to Paris, and that there, to convince the most incredulous of the great results obtained, they should march along the boulevards and past the Column Vendôme.

3

The Second Fortnight of February

At the beginning of the second fortnight of February Napoleon was far from despairing of his chances. Still, the defeat of the army of Silesia was only an episode, not a final solution. He now had to contend with the Austrian army commanded by the Prince of Schwarzenberg, who, after having forced the bridges of Nogent, Bray, and Montereau, was advancing on Nangis. The Bavarians, under General von Wrede, and the Russians, under General Wittgenstein, formed the vanguard. The Austrian corps of Bianchi was marching on Fontainebleau, while Platow's Cossacks were devastating the region between the Yonne and the Loire. Napoleon reached Meaux February 15, and the next day moved towards Guignes. The road was covered with carts, into which the neighbouring villagers crowded a durable supply of provisions for the weary soldiers. The artillery advanced in post-wagons.

The same day the Parisians read in the *Moniteur:* "The exasperation of the inhabitants is at its height. The enemy is everywhere committing the most horrible outrages. All the measures are taken for surrounding them on every side at the first movement in retreat. Thousands await only this moment to rise. The sacred soil which the enemy have polluted will be their grave. This army of Silesia, composed of the Russian corps of Sachen and Langeron, and Kleist's and York's Prussian corps, and consisting of eighty thousand men, has been beaten, scattered, annihilated, in four days."

February 18 the *Moniteur* contained this article: "The atrocities committed by the Cossacks pass all conception. In their wild intoxication they have offered violence to women of sixty and girls of twelve. The peasants, in their eagerness for vengeance, guided by invalided soldiers, and armed with the guns of the enemy picked up on the battlefield, have laid hands on all they have met. Those armies which boasted that they had entered our territory to bring peace, happiness, science, and arts, will meet with destruction."

Napoleon had slept at Nangis February 17. In the evening a flag of truce appeared at the outposts. It was Count von Paar, who asked for an armistice in the name of Prince Schwarzenberg. The next day Napoleon wrote to Joseph:—

My Brother: Prince Schwarzenberg has just shown a sign of life. He has sent a flag of truce to ask for a suspension of hostilities. It is not easy to be so cowardly. Constantly he had refused in the most insulting terms every form of the suspension of hostilities, of armistice, even the reception of my flags of truce, after the battles of Dantzic and of Dresden,—a horrible thing, almost unheard of in history. These wretches fall on their knees at the first reverse. Fortunately Prince Schwarzenberg's *aide-de-camp* was denied entrance. I have only received his letter, which I shall answer at my convenience.

I shall grant no armistice until they have evacuated my territory. From what I hear, everything has altered with the Allies. The Emperor of Russia, who a few days ago broke off negotiations because he wished to impose on France severer conditions than her old boundaries, now desires to renew them; and I hope soon to make a peace on the Frankfort basis, which is the least that I can do with honour. Before beginning operations I offered to sign a treaty accepting the old boundaries, provided they would stop at once.

This step was taken by the. Duke of Vicenza on the 8th. They answered in the negative, alleging that even signing the preliminaries would not put a stop to hostilities, which could only happen when all the articles of peace were signed. This inconceivable reply has been punished; and yesterday, the 17th, they begged for an armistice! You may imagine that, being, on the eve of a battle in which I was determined to conquer or to perish, and in which, if I were beaten, my capital would have been taken, I agreed to anything to avoid this terrible risk.

I owed to my family and to my people this sacrifice of my pride; but when they refused it, and the risk of battle was renewed and the chances of ordinary war returned, in which my capital was no longer imperilled by a single battle, and everything was in my favour, I owe it to the interest of the Empire and to my own glory to negotiate a real peace. If I had signed with the old boundaries, I should have renewed the war in two years, telling the nation that it was not a peace that I had signed, but a capitulation. In the new state of affairs I should not be able to say it, since now that fortune is once more favourable to me I am master of the conditions.

Was this optimism sincere? Was Napoleon trying to deceive others or to deceive himself? However this may be, the end of the letter seems to show great confidence in the future. "The enemy," he said, "is in a very different condition from that in which it was when the Frankfort conditions were proposed and is convinced that but few of its troops will again cover the frontiers. The cavalry is very tired and dispirited; the infantry worn out by marching and countermarching, and thoroughly discouraged. Hence I hope to be able to make a peace such as every reasonable man could desire; and my desires do not go beyond the Frankfort propositions. Spread it abroad that the enemy has asked for an armistice or a suspension of hostilities; an absurd request, because it would rob me of the advantages I had gained by my manoeuvres; add that this shows their discouragement. Don't let it be printed, but have it said everywhere."

February 18, the day this letter was written, Napoleon was

victorious at the battle of Montereau, one of the most brilliant affairs of the campaign. Never had he shown greater audacity. Recalling his training in the artillery, he aimed the guns himself, ordered the firing, and when the men murmured at the rash way in which he exposed himself, he exclaimed: "Don't worry, my friends; the ball that is going to kill me isn't yet cast." February 19, he wrote to Joseph from the castle of Surville:—

> My Brother: It took us all day to get through that horrible pass of Montereau. I have just had a bridge thrown over the Seine, and another over the Yonne. The Emperor of Russia and the King of Prussia were at Bray. As soon as they heard that I had won the bridge of Montereau, they fled in all haste. The enemy's army is terrified. The three sovereigns have been for some days at Pont, at *Madame's*. They expected to reach Fontainebleau tomorrow, and to be at Paris in a few days.
>
> Everything that has befallen them seems inconceivable. Today is cold, and snow is falling. I send to the Empress something for the *Moniteur,* but you might have put in the *Moniteur,* and small newspapers, under news from the Provinces, an article about the haste in which the sovereigns left Bray. The Austrians have guaranteed my palace of Fontainebleau against the pillage of the Cossacks. I could not be more satisfied with the spirit displayed by all the towns and the country, and by the feelings of every one.

In Paris, hope began to revive. Joseph wrote to the Emperor, February 20:

> Your Majesty has every reason to believe that his wishes for an honourable peace on the Frankfort condition will be granted. I do not believe that there is a single Frenchman with different opinions;

and February 21:

> Everyone agrees that Your Majesty should not have accorded a suspension of hostilities. Every one desires peace

with the natural boundaries. No one now wants the former frontiers.

February 20, Napoleon has advanced up the Seine, on the left bank, by the road from Montereau to Nogent. That evening he halted in this last town, which had suffered cruelly, and was but a mass of burnt and battered walls. In this disaster the Sisters of Saint Vincent de Paul had, as ever, performed miracles of devotion and charity. The Emperor thanked them in the name of the country. Meanwhile the retreat of the enemy after the reverse at Montereau seemed to be turning into a rout. A sort of panic threw disorder into their ranks. The roads through the Vosges were lined with carts, drivers, wounded, and fugitives, hurrying to the Rhine. A hundred thousand men were fleeing before Napoleon, who had but forty thousand for their pursuit.

It was then—February 21, 1814—that he wrote from Nogent to his father-in-law, the Emperor of Austria, one of the most curious letters that ever came from his pen. It began thus:—

My Brother and very dear Father-in-law: I did my best to avoid the battle which has just taken place. Fortune has favoured me, and I have destroyed the Russian and Prussian army commanded by General Blücher, and later, the Prussian army commanded by General Kleist. In this state of affairs, whatever opinions may exist at your headquarters, my army outnumbers in infantry, cavalry, and artillery Your Majesty's army. And if this assurance should be necessary to your decision, I shall have no difficulty in proving this to any man of sound judgment, such as Prince Schwarzenberg, Count Bubna, or Prince Metternich.

I deem it my duty to write to Your Majesty, because this contest between a French army and one mainly Austrian seems to me contrary to your interests as well as to my own. If fortune betrays my hopes, Your Majesty's situation will be only the more embarrassing. If I defeat your army, how will it withdraw from France with the population already exasperated to the highest pitch by the crimes of all sorts of which the Cossacks and the Russians have been guilty? In this state of affairs, I propose to Your Majesty to sign a peace without delay, on the bases you proposed at Frankfort, which I and the French nation have adopted as our ultimatum.

I say more: these bases can alone re-establish the European equilibrium. If harder conditions had been imposed on France, peace would have been of short duration. There is no Frenchman who would not have preferred death to the acceptance of conditions which could make us slaves of England, and strike out France from the list of powers. England may well desire to destroy Antwerp, and to put an obstacle in the way of the re-establishment of the French navy; but you, Sire, what is your interest in the annihilation of the French navy? Your Majesty becomes a maritime power by the conditions you set at Frankfort. Do you want your flag outraged and insulted by England as it constantly has been?

What interest can Your Majesty have in putting Belgium under the yoke of a Protestant prince, whose son will ascend the English throne? All these hopes and plans lie beyond the power of the Coalition. If the battle against Your Majesty's army should be lost, I have the means for fighting two more before it reaches Paris; and even if Paris were taken, the rest of France would never endure the yoke proposed in this treaty, which seems to be inspired by the English policy.

The convulsion of the nation would augment its energy and its forces fourfold. I shall never cede Antwerp and Belgium. If Your Majesty persists in abandoning his proper interests for the policy of England or the resentment of Russia, and will only lay down arms on the frightful conditions proposed at the Congress, the genius of France and Providence will be on our side. The Emperor Alexander's thirst for vengeance has no good ground. I offered him peace before entering Moscow; at Moscow, I did my best to extinguish the fire started by his orders. Besides, in Paris two hundred thousand men are under arms; they have learned by the actions of the Russians, the emptiness of their promises; they know what fate they would have to expect.

I ask Your Majesty to avoid the risks of battle. I ask peace, a prompt peace, based on the proclamation which Prince Schwarzenberg published as the Declaration of the Allied Powers, inserted in the *Frankfort Journal,* the bases that I have accepted, and accept again, although the position of the Allies is very different from what it was then, and now any impartial man will agree that the chances are on my side.

This really eloquent letter, breathing a combination of pain and pride, closes with a pathetic appeal to the heart of the father of Marie Louise, the grandfather of the King of Rome. The Emperor does not mention his wife or his son by name; yet they appear as if they were carrying an olive branch. It was not family feeling alone that was invoked. Napoleon reminded the ruler of Austria that he was head of the house of Lorraine, that his blood was French blood. This is the end of the letter, which deeply moved Emperor Francis and nearly saved France:

May I be allowed to say to Your Majesty that in spite of all you have done against me since the invasion of my territory, and the faint memory you preserve of the ties that unite us, and of the relations which our states are called upon to maintain for their common interest, my feelings are unchanged, and I cannot observe with indifference that if you refuse peace, this refusal will bring misery to your life and many evils to all, while a single word of yours can put an end to everything, bring about a reconciliation, and restore to the world, and especially to Europe, lasting tranquillity.

If I could have been cowardly enough to accept the conditions of the English and Russian ministers, you ought to have dissuaded me, because you knew that nothing that disgraces thirty millions of men can be durable. Your Majesty can put an end to this war by a single word, can assure the happiness of his own people and of Europe, secure himself against the fickleness of fortune, and terminate the evils of a nation, the prey not of ordinary sufferings, but of the crimes of the Tartars of the desert, who scarcely deserve to be called men.

I take it for granted that Your Majesty has not to ask me why I write to him. I cannot address the English, whose policy it is to destroy my navy, or to the Emperor Alexander, since passion and revenge inspire all his feelings. Hence, I can write to Your Majesty alone, my recent ally, who, by the strength of his army and the extent of his empire, is regarded as the leading force of the Coalition; in short, to Your Majesty, who, whatever his feelings at the moment, has French blood flowing in his veins.

Napoleon was untiring. His pen was as active as his sword. No detail escaped his vigilance. He was everywhere, seeing to everything at once. The very day he wrote to the Emperor of Austria, he sent this letter to Joseph:—

My Brother: You ought to have no anxiety about Orleans and Montargis. The movement I am making will attract the enemy very speedily, and their corps will be glad to fall back promptly. I think it would be well for the Regent to write to the city of Orleans in some such way as this: 'I learn that the city of Orleans is threatened by fifteen hundred scouts of the enemy's army. What! The city of Orléans, with forty thousand inhabitants, is afraid of fifteen hundred cavalry! Where is the French energy? Form your National Guard, organise a company of artillery, take from your stables the necessary horses.

'I give orders to the Minister of War to supply you with twelve cannon and five howitzers for the defence of your city and property. The enemy who threatens us is implac-

31

able; he ravages our countryside and sacks our cities; he has not kept a single one of his promises. To arms, then, inhabitants of Orleans, and confirm by your actions the opinion I have formed of you and of the French nation!' A number of such letters, signed by the Empress, would have more effect than signed by me.

I think that the Empress might write to Lille, Valenciennes, Cambrai, and other large towns near the northern frontier in similar terms, modifying the language according to the zeal these towns have shown in recent events. It would be well for the Empress to write them all with her own hand. I think, too, that a proclamation to Belgium, from the Empress as Regent, would be of use. This proclamation might be put into the form of a letter to the mayor of Brussels, the mayor of Ghent, of Bruges, of Mons, etc. The Empress might make mention of the successes I have had, of the desire of the English to detach them from France and to bring them under the yoke of a prince who has always been hostile to their country and their religion; soon the enemy will be convinced that no peace will be signed in which the Allies do not guarantee France the integrity of its natural boundaries. These letters might be expressed differently to make them seem like different proclamations."

Napoleon made superhuman exertions to arouse the patriotism of the French, but he had to deal with a country so exhausted and discouraged that his heroism and that of the army were powerless. Joseph wrote to his brother February 22:

The feeling at Toulouse and Bordeaux is very bad, and a Bourbon would be received if he should present himself. I suppose that we are on the eve of a battle. Whatever may be the result, the present state of things cannot last. The administration is everywhere falling into decay, money is lacking, and the system of making requisitions is finally deadening all zeal and isolating the government. However harsh these facts are, since Your Majesty cannot hear them from the lips of his Ministers, I do not hesitate to assume the painful task of uttering them.

As to the National Guard of Paris, it would have been a great mistake to place any dependence upon it. King Joseph in the same letter spoke about it in this way: "The National Guard, in its present condition, is a security against anarchy; it means well; it has been aroused by hearing of the miracles Your Majesty has wrought in a few days; it is anxious for a peace that shall bring you back to your capital, and is inclined to love as well as to admiration. This feeling is shared by the whole city, but to say more, Sire, would be false and would mislead Your Majesty.

This city of Paris, so hostile to the government a month ago, so touched by Your Majesty's confidence as shown by your entrusting to it your wife and son, so encouraged and amazed by Your Majesty's successes, nevertheless is not in a state from which it is possible to expect fidelity or obedience. It has admired your genius; but it can only be moved to enthusiasm by the hope of a speedy peace, and is not at all disposed to undertake any serious defence against a single army corps, or to send outside of the city any detachments of the National Guard. That, Sire, is the exact truth. Your Majesty must not count on any effort beyond what may be expected from a populace thus disposed.

So far from losing heart, Napoleon became more confident every day. He hoped that the general uprising of the frontier provinces, the sorties of the garrisons, Augereau's attack on the rear of the Austrian army, would turn the Allies' retreat beyond the Rhine into a hopeless rout. In his delight at seeing them retreat before him in the direction of Troyes, he felt all his pride return when in the morning of February 23, within the four bare walls of the hovel of a wheelwright of the village of Châtre, where he had passed the night, he received the visit of Prince Wentzel Lichtenstein, an *aide-de-camp* of Prince Schwarzenberg, who brought him propositions for an armistice.

The language of the Austrian envoy was not merely peaceful; it expressed a deference and an admiration which highly flattered the Emperor. Then he said to the *aide-de-camp* of Prince Schwarzenberg:

> So the favourite plan of England has prevailed in the counsels of the Coalition. Their war has become a personal one. It was decidedly against my dynasty that it was aimed.

Prince Lichtenstein having protested against this supposition, Napoleon spoke to him of the connivance of the Allies with the intrigues of the Duke of Angoulême, of the Duke of Berry, of Count d'Artois, and showed some surprise at seeing the Emperor of Austria working to dethrone his own daughter. At this the Prince exclaimed:

> Such an intention would be unnatural. My august sovereign, the Emperor, would never lend himself to it. As to the presence of the Bourbons, it is to be regarded as a means of war, to secure a peace which my mission proves is desired.

This answer filled Napoleon with joy, and he promised that an armistice should be arranged. He fancied that he had returned to the grand days of his power and glory. After Prince Lichtenstein had gone he was overheard exclaiming in an outburst of pride:

> The Allies will repent their insolence. They will see that I am nearer their capitals than they are to mine. Yes, we are nearer Munich than they are to Paris.

The next day, February 24, he entered Troyes, which the enemy had just evacuated; a flag of truce brought him word that Lusigny, near Vandœuvres, had been chosen for the negotiation of the armistice. In his talk with the messenger he said loudly: "I am nearer Vienna than you are to Paris."

The *Moniteur* gave an account of the Emperor's entrance into the capital of Champagne:

It is impossible to form an idea of the annoyances to which the inhabitants have been exposed during the seventeen days that the enemy have occupied the city. It would also be hard to describe the enthusiasm and eagerness they displayed over the arrival of the Emperor. A mother who sees her children saved from death, slaves who see their chains broken after the crudest captivity, know no keener joy than that shown by the people of Troyes. Their conduct has been honourable and praiseworthy. The theatre was open every evening, but not a man, or a woman, of even the lower classes, was willing to be present. The whole populace is eager to march.

Intoxicated by his success, Napoleon wrote to Joseph this letter overflowing with pride:—

My Brother: I am at Troyes. The enemy's army pursues me with flags of truce, asking for a suspension of hostilities. I have had many cavalry skirmishes. I have captured two thousand prisoners and cannon. I am writing to the Empress to have thirty guns fired, both for these minor affairs and for the deliverance of the capital of Champagne. If I had had twenty skiffs to cross the Seine when I wanted, there would have been no Austrian army left. However, there is great terror in the enemy's ranks.

A few days ago they thought I had no army; now there is no limit to what they imagine: three or four hundred thousand men are not enough. Formerly they thought I had no reserves; now they say I have massed all my veterans and face them only with picked troops. That is what fear does. It is important that the Paris newspapers should confirm this alarm.

The Minister of the Interior is a poltroon; he has a foolish idea of men. Neither he nor the Minister of Police has any more idea of France than I have of China. The enemy has committed so many atrocities that France will be indignant. Here, on the spot, the most moderate cannot speak of them calmly. If the French were as despicable as the Ministry of the Interior seems to think, I should myself blush to be a Frenchman.

General de Ségur, the historian of this drama of the invasion, in which he took a part, says that at this moment fortune hung on a single thread; a little more and the Coalition would have fallen by its own weight, and France would have been saved. Napoleon's frequent blows upon the Marne, his reappearance on the banks of the Seine, the massing of an army at Lyons, seemed to make the enemy lose their head. General de Ségur adds:

Pozzo di Borgo, the bitterest of Napoleon's personal enemies, the Corsican who turned Russian, whose hate had most encouraged the Allies to push on the war to the end, has often affirmed this to us. How often has he described to us all the invective which succeeded the high consideration he had acquired by the success of his advice! With the exception of the Prussians, the enemy's staffs, in their alarm at finding themselves so far in France, imagined that they were caught in a snare.

This minister had become the object of universal reprobation. Emperor Alexander told him that they had done enough; that a victorious march from Moscow to the banks of the Seine was sufficient; that they should not expose their advantages to a second day of Marengo; that evidently Napoleon was growing stronger with the aid of France. Were they not finding in him once more the general of the Army of Italy?

The alarmists in the allied camp said that their retreat would be a repetition of the retreat from Russia, and all that Napoleon heard about their panic filled him with one of the greatest joys he had ever known.

In Paris, Sunday, February 27, the flags which had recently been captured by the Emperor, were formally presented to the Empress Regent. They were borne by two officers of the Imperial Guard, four officers of troops of the line, and four officers of the National Guard, who started from the Ministry of War and proceeded with the Ministers to the Tuileries, with a band in front and an escort following. The Minister of War said to Marie Louise:

Madame: When the Saracens were defeated by Charles Martel in the plains of Tours and Poitiers, the capital was decked with the spoils of but a single nation. Today, when dangers no less serious than those then threatening France have produced more important and more difficult successes, your august spouse presents to you these banners captured from the three great powers of Europe. Since a blind hate has stirred up against us so many nations, even those to whom France had restored their independence, for which she has made great sacrifices, may it not be said that these flags are captured from all Europe?

These pledges of French valour are for us the tokens of new and still greater successes, if the enemy's obstinacy prolongs the war. This noble hope fills the heart of every Frenchman. You share it, *Madame*, you who, ever trusting in your august husband's genius, in the love and energy of the nation, have continued to show, in all the circumstances of this war, a firmness of soul and virtues worthy of the admiration of Europe and of posterity.

Marie Louise replied:

Duke of Feltre, Minister of War: It is with keen emotion that I see these trophies which you present to me in obedience to the orders of the Emperor, my august spouse. To my eyes they are the pledges of the safety of the country. At the sight of them may all the French rise in arms! May they throng about their monarch and their father! Their courage, led by his genius, will soon have accomplished the deliverance of our territory.

At the end of the audience, the fourteen flags—one Austrian, four Prussian, and nine Russian—were carried with great pomp to the Invalides. Cavalry rode at the head and at the end of the procession.

At this moment Marie Louise felt hope revive. She could not imagine that she would be abandoned by her father, and fancied that her anxieties would soon be over. The evening before, she had written to Emperor Francis a really touching letter from which she expected the best results. In it she said:

It is not good policy to force a disgraceful peace upon us, for it cannot last. Imagine, dear father, in what a state I am. For me it would be a blow I could not survive. Hence I beseech you, dear father, to remember me and my son. You know how much I love you, and how much I flatter myself that I enjoy your fatherly affection.

The Empress went on to say that the condition of affairs and her husband's absence were affecting her health. "It depends on you," she closed, "to put an end to my anxiety. You will do this, won't you?"

Marie Louise saw about her less gloomy faces than a few days before. The courtiers, who had kept aloof, began to reappear, and to speak with enthusiasm of the Emperor's genius. They said that the dynasty was unattackable, and that it would have been a disgrace to accept the boundaries of 1792; that they were going to have the natural boundaries, that the request for armistice was a sign of an early peace, which would be as honourable for France as for its glorious ruler. The Empress gladly listened to these flattering words, and at the end of February there prevailed at the Tuileries a feeling of tranquillity which was, alas! To be of but brief duration.

Blücher, that obstinate and implacable enemy, was about to change the face of things. While the bulk of the French army was massed about Troyes, thinking of the armistice and the peace, the Prussian troops were rapidly advancing on both banks of the Marne in the direction of Paris. Napoleon received word of this in the night of February 26. The morning of the 27th he suddenly started from Troyes to pursue the Prussian army through

Arcis-sur-Aube and Sézanne. The evening of that day he took up his quarters at Herbisse, in the house of a simple country priest. The officers spent the night on chairs, tables, or straw. In spite of the serious condition of things they preserved all their jollity, in the hope that this new march on the flank of the Prussian army would be as fruitful as the other.

The situation, however, at once complicated itself most seriously. The Austrians had suddenly resumed the offensive at the very moment when Napoleon left Troyes. It was expected that they would be pursued to the Rhine, and they were rallying between Langres and Bar. Marshal Augereau could no longer make the diversion on the Saône. Blücher's army, threatening Paris, was already at the gates of Meaux, and in front of it there were only the insufficient forces of Marmont and Mortier. Nevertheless, the Emperor was not disturbed; at first he had hopes of ridding himself of Blücher after he had made a junction with the two marshals, then to return on the Seine soon enough to stop the Austrians and save Troyes. His troops, exhausted by fatigue, but yet full of ardour, advanced by forced marches on Ferté-sous-Jouarre. It was the end of February. Events were crowding on one another; everyone felt that the end of the drama was not far off.

4

The First Fortnight of March

The first fortnight of March was for Napoleon a period of anguish even more terrible than the previous weeks. After profiting so long by what he called his star, he found himself face to face with an evil fate which paralysed every effort of his genius. An absolutely unexpected accident—the capitulation of Soissons—suddenly overthrew his profoundest combinations, and swept all his pieces from the board. Nevertheless, hoping against hope, he continued the struggle, facing misfortune with an energy hardly equalled in history. His pride, far from diminishing, only became greater.

The darker fortune became, the more he yearned to control it. He tried to inspire, not pity, but fear. He wrote to his ministers and spoke to his generals in the old imperious tone which had marked the days of his greatest power. In his presence no one dared to utter a murmur, for his personal ascendancy was still irresistible; but behind his back there was much denunciation of his boundless ambition, the main cause of the woes of France. The feeling of the army continued admirable, but in Paris the discouragement was profound. There anything seemed preferable to war, and even in official circles nothing was demanded but an immediate cessation of hostilities, even with the loss of the natural frontiers, the glorious conquest of the Republic.

The great nation, always accustomed to attacking, could not reconcile itself to the idea of defence. It was timidly whispered that in spite of all the optimistic announcements and the many bulletins of victories, the enemy was only a few leagues from the capital, and the great majority of Parisians felt none of the ardour and fanaticism of the defenders of Saragossa or of those who burned Moscow. Marie Louise felt isolated, shorn of support, deprived of counsellors, and more like a victim than a sovereign. King Joseph appeared more terrified than ever; no one in the Empress's court spoke a word of encouragement. The faint gleam of hope which for a moment lit up the situation vanished at once. The courtiers, who had worn a cheerful face for two or three days, were again plunged in gloom, and every one at the Tuileries was oppressed by a presentiment of the impending catastrophe.

Nevertheless, at the beginning of March Napoleon was still full of hope. In the night of the 2nd his troops, full of ardour, effected the crossing of the Marne. Blücher's soldiers, with the Aisne before them, the Marne in their rear, threatened on the left by the troops of the Duke of Treviso and the Duke of Ragusa, on the right by Napoleon's army, imagined that all was lost, but at the very moment when they were about to be driven back on Soissons and doubtless compelled to lay down their arms under the walls of this city, an unexpected piece of good fortune saved them.

Soissons, which, although occupied by a garrison of but one thousand men, could have held out twenty-four hours longer and so have given Napoleon time to arrive, was surrendered March 3 by its commander, General Moreau, who was in no way related to the other great general of the same name. Bülow and Wintzengerode, coming, one from Belgium, the other from Luxembourg, joined Blücher, raising his army from fifty thousand to a hundred and ten thousand men, and Soissons, instead of being his ruin, was his salvation.

Napoleon was at Fismes, March 4, when he heard the fatal news. He exclaimed in anguish:

> I had that madman of a Blücher in the arms of the Aisne, and now they have surrendered Soissons and given him the bridge without blowing it up! It's that wretched Moreau

who has ruined us! That name is fatal to France.

Hubert, one of the Emperor's valets, said:

From that day my master's face continually wore a look of
melancholy, even of unhappiness. I looked in vain for that
kind and amiable smile which formerly lent his often terrible expression a touching grace, which one remembered
as if it were a kindness or a most pleasing reward. From
that time his smile was forced and painful: his voice, his
every action, was marked with sadness.

The day that the Emperor learned of the surrender of Soissons, which upset all his plans, Marie Louise was presiding at the
Tuileries over an extraordinary council charged with the examination of the conditions of peace proposed by the Allies at the
Congress of Châtillon. These conditions comprised the restoration of the old boundaries to France, and, with one exception,
all the members of the council agreed to accept them.

"Rigorous as the treaty was," says the Duke of Rovigo, "it
preserved in France the established government, and maintained
the existence of the Emperor and his family. England recognized
the new dynasty,—an advantage which none of the previous
negotiations had accorded to Napoleon. There was no question
of the Bourbons, who appeared to have been abandoned. This
was a great thing for the Emperor, who thereby found himself
better treated than even France."

What the Ministers and high dignitaries most desired was
to preserve their own places; hence all agreed in condemning
a resistance which seemed hopeless. The very day when this
council was held with the Empress presiding, Joseph wrote to
his brother:

It is generally agreed that it is better to accept the boundaries as they were in 1792, than to expose the capital. The
occupation of the capital, it is thought, would be the end of
the existing order, and the beginning of great misfortunes.
Allied Europe wishes to reduce France to what it was in

1792; this may well be the basis of a treaty commanded by circumstances, but let the territory be evacuated at once. In short, a speedy peace, of any sort, is indispensable. It will be a two or three years' truce, but, good or bad, we must have peace. The natural boundaries would be a real benefit for France and for Europe; they would give hope of a long peace, but no one is held by an impossibility. So make a truce *in petto,* since the injustice of the enemy does not allow a just peace, and the state of feeling and of affairs permits no hope that France will make efforts proportionate to the object to be aimed at. Your letter, to the Emperor of Austria is thought to be noble and reasonable. You will stay in France; France will remain what she was when it astounded Europe; and you who saved it once will save it again, by signing this peace, and save yourself as well.

Be recognized by England; deliver France from the Cossacks and the Prussians, and some day France will make up to you in blessings what superficial people will imagine that you have lost in glory.

Napoleon, above all things a warrior, had a horror of a peace which seemed to him disgraceful. Even after the surrender of Soissons, he hoped to possess the natural frontiers of France. The enormous numerical superiority of Blücher's forces did not prevent his pursuing the Prussians and the Russians beyond the Aisne, and March 7 he fought the bloody battle of Craonne.

Here the French had to take by assault a lofty plateau, defended by fifty thousand men and a full supply of artillery, while the attacking force consisted of but thirty thousand, with insufficient artillery. The enemy withdrew in good order towards Laon and prepared for a second battle. Napoleon followed them. To the hundred thousand experienced troops of his adversary he could oppose only thirty thousand, young, sick, and ill-equipped.

These boys, these creatures of a day, as General de Ségur called them, who had joined one evening to be sacrificed on the morrow, could scarcely be styled soldiers. One day General Drouot, seeing them so young, so frail, half-clad, ill-trained, fighting one against four, said emphatically, that it was "a repetition of the slaughter of the innocents.

Nevertheless, Napoleon continued the struggle with a sort of fury. At Laon he fought a second and terrible battle, which continued for two days, the 9th and 10th of March, but in spite of his heroic exertions, he was compelled to retreat on Soissons, which he entered on the 12th in profound dejection.

Joseph had written to him, March 9:

> After the new victory you have gained [that of Craonne] you can sign with glory peace with the former boundaries. This peace will restore France to itself after the long conflict which begun in 1792, and will contain nothing to its dishonour, since it will have lost none of its old territory, and will have made the interior changes it desired. As for you, Sire, so often victorious, I am convinced that you have within you all that is necessary to make the French forget, or rather to remember, what was best in the government of Louis XII., Henri IV., and Louis XIV., if you make a firm peace with Europe, and follow the natural instincts of your kind character, renouncing what is factitious and consenting to live as a great king after flourishing as a great man. When you have saved France from anarchy and from the coalition of all Europe, you will become the father of your people, and will be adored as much as Louis XII., after having been more adored than Henri IV. and Louis XIV.; and to secure so many kinds of glory, you have only to wish your own happiness and that of France.

Joseph's wise and fraternal counsel appeared to Napoleon like satirical reprimand. Having always chosen to inspire fear rather than love, he hated to think that after having been the greatest of conquerors, he could henceforth be only a kindly monarch, a simple father of his people. He distrusted his brother, as he did every one, and regarded him as a petty creature void of courage,—indeed, he doubted the disinterestedness of his advice. There had been imprudent talk in the suite of the former King of Spain. Men who had never seen a battlefield said of the Emperor: "He is a madman; he will have us all killed." It was even insinuated that a new regency would have to be formed, with Joseph at the head, because he was a pacific and moderate Prince with whom Europe would treat more willingly than with Napoleon. The echo of many of their words reached Napoleon's ears, and the wounded but always terrible lion rose in his might. This Jupiter Tonans was, perhaps, haughtier even than at the time when his slightest frown sent a shudder through the Olympus of emperors and kings.

He would not even admit the idea that he might have need of his wife to escape from the dangers against which he was struggling. He wrote to Joseph from Soissons, March 12, 1814:

> I am sorry to see that you have been talking to my wife about the Bourbons and the opposition the Emperor of Austria might make to them. I beg of you to avoid these conversations. I do not wish to be protected by my wife; this idea would spoil her, and divide us. What is the use of such talk? Let her lead her own life; speak to her only about what she must know in order to affix her signature; and above all, avoid everything that could make her think I desire to be protected by her or her father. Not once for four years has the word Bourbon or Austria crossed my lips. Besides, all that can only disturb her and injure her excellent character.
>
> You always write as if peace depended on me; but I sent you all the documents. If the Parisians want to see the Cossacks, they will repent it; but, once more, must the truth out? I have never sought the applause of the Parisians. I am not a performer in an opera. Besides, you would need to be much more practical than you are to understand the feeling of that city, which has nothing in common with the passions of the three or four thousand people who make so much noise. It is perfectly simple, and much quicker, to say that it is impossible to make a levy

of men than to try to make one. The Emperor of Austria is powerless, because he is weak, and is led by Metternich, who is in the pay of England: that's the whole secret.

The evening before, Joseph had written a letter which added to the Emperor's irritation. It contained the following passages:

The upshot of all that has been said to me by the Ministers, the officers of the National Guard, of all that I know of the persons attached to the existing order, is that peace is forced upon us by the nature of things. There is not a man who would not loudly crave it, were it not for fear of displeasing you; and in fact, it is only your enemies who would dissuade you from accepting peace with the former frontiers. Disturbing rumours are beginning to make their way through the capital, which tend to cast discredit on Your Majesty. For example, they speak of the recall of the Duke of Conegliano, who is much loved.

March is passing, and the fields are not sown. But it is unnecessary to go into details. Your Majesty must feel that there is no remedy but peace, and a speedy peace. Every day lost does us personally much harm; private misery is very great, and there is no doubt that whenever the conviction is established that Your Majesty prefers the continuance of the war to a peace (however disgraceful), weariness will turn men's minds in the contrary direction. If Toulouse and Bordeaux protect a Bourbon, you will have civil war, and the vast population of Paris will favour the one who will secure the earlier peace.

Napoleon answered this letter as follows;

Soissons, March 12, 1814: Everywhere I hear the complaints of the people against their mayors and the middle classes who prevent their defending themselves: I see the same thing in Paris. The people have energy and honour. I am very much afraid that there are certain leaders who do not wish to fight and who will be much disturbed, after all is over, by what will have happened to them.

The untiring soldier would not confess himself beaten by fate. His inconceivable audacity had so impressed Blücher that the obstinate Prussian kept his troops motionless for a week. Napoleon took advantage of this respite to reorganize his feeble army, to put garrisons in Compigne in a condition to defend themselves, and to retake Rheims, after a battle in which there fell General de Saint Priest, a French *émigré* who had a position in the Russian army. March 14, the Emperor wrote to Joseph:—

My Brother: Yesterday I reached Rheims, which General de Saint Priest had occupied with three Russian divisions and a new Prussian division which had come from the blockade of Stettin. I beat them, recapturing the city, twenty cannon, and many stores. General de Saint Priest was mortally wounded; his leg was amputated at the thigh. What is strange is, that Saint Priest was wounded by the same artilleryman that killed General Moreau. One must say, O Providence! O Providence!

Napoleon at Rheims, in the shadow of the great cathedral in which the kings of France were formerly crowned, still proudly enjoyed his position as sovereign. He could not listen to a word of criticism or of advice, and, March 14, he wrote to Joseph this letter which shows all the haughtiness of his character:—

My Brother: I am sorry you have told the Duke of Conegliano what I wrote to you. I don't like this gossiping. If it suited my views to order the Duke of Conegliano elsewhere, the chatter of Paris would not move me. The National Guard of Paris forms part of the French people, and so long as I live I shall be master everywhere in France. Your character and mine are very different. You like to coax people and to follow their ideas, while I require to be pleased and to have people obey mine. Today, as at Austerlitz, I am master. Don't let anyone wheedle the

National Guard, or let Regnaud or anyone else become their tribune. I suppose, however, that they perceive the difference between the time of La Fayette, when the people were sovereign, and now, when I am. I have prepared a decree to raise twelve battalions by a general levy. The execution of this measure is not to be impeded in any way whatsoever. If the people perceive that instead of doing what is necessary, there is any effort to please them, it will be natural for them to think themselves sovereign and to form a poor idea of those who govern them.

The same day Napoleon wrote to the Duke of Rovigo, Minister of Police, this still more imperious letter:

You tell me nothing of what is going on in Paris. They are talking about an address, the Regency, and a thousand intrigues as silly as they are absurd, which can only be devised by a simpleton like Miot. These people seem not to know that I cut the gordian knot like Alexander. They must know that I am today the same man I was at Wagram and Austerlitz, that I desire no intrigue in the country, that there is no authority there but mine, and that in case of confusion the Regent alone possesses my confidence. King Joseph is weak; he busies himself with intrigues which might be' fatal to the state, and certainly to himself and to his counsel, if he does not speedily return to the right path.

I am displeased to learn all this from another source than yourself. Understand that if there had been made an address contrary to the constituted authority, I should have had the King, my Ministers, and all who signed it, arrested. The National Guard is spoiled, Paris is spoiled, by weakness and ignorance of the country. I wish no tribune of the people. Remember it is I who am the grand tribune; then the people will always do what suits its real interests, which are the object of all my thoughts.

During the three days which the Emperor spent at Rheims,

the 14th, 15th, and 10th of March, 1814, he was much more a monarch than a general, and he busied himself with the internal affairs of the Empire as carefully as if it had been at peace. Very striking is the authoritative tone which marked all his words and letters to the very end of the campaign, even to "his abdication. Nothing had discouraged him. It was in vain that the forces of the Coalition grew while his own dwindled; in vain that he received from Paris the most alarming news; in vain that he saw treachery encompassing him on every side like a rising tide; he looked at danger with a fearless eye, and still braved fortune, which had so long been the humblest of his slaves.

5

The Châtillon Congress

The Congress of Châtillon was drawing to an end, and the plenipotentiaries of France, England, Austria, Prussia, and Russia were about to separate without having been able to accomplish anything in the way of peace. Before we go on with the study of the military events, let us take a glance at this fruitless effort of diplomacy. All its phases we have studied in the archives of the Ministry of Foreign Affairs, and most of the documents that we shall cite have never been printed.

It is our impression that if Napoleon could have contented himself with the frontiers of 1792, he would have saved his crown; but he desired the natural boundaries of France, and the Allies were absolutely determined to refuse them. Consequently the negotiations moved in a vicious circle, and all the arguments of the plenipotentiaries were but a futile war of words.

At times Napoleon seemed disposed to yield, but as soon as he achieved any success in the field, he tossed his head and rejected with scorn what he regarded as insulting propositions. At the beginning, the efforts of diplomacy had filled loyal Frenchmen with hope, and the traitors with fear, for the traitors would have preferred the ruin of Napoleon to the safety of France; soon, however, it became clear that the voice of the plenipotentiaries was drowned by the roar of cannon and that the tremendous conflict of France with Europe was to be ended, not by the pen, but by the sword.

The Congress which had met at Châtillon-sur-Seine, in the

department of Côte-d'Or, close to the scene of war, seemed an irony of fate. Surprise was felt that fighting and negotiation should be going on simultaneously, and the diplomatists, who were treating one another with perfect courtesy, while their fellow-countrymen were slaughtering one another, produced a singular effect in this terrible drama.

France had but one plenipotentiary to contend alone with Count Stadion, the Austrian representative, Count Rasumovski, the Russian; von Humboldt, the Prussian; and the three English plenipotentiaries, Lord Cathcart, Sir Charles Stuart, and Lord Aberdeen. This sole representative of France was General de Caulaincourt, Duke of Vicenza, a brave soldier, a man of honour, a sturdy patriot. It is easy to imagine what he must have suffered in maintaining his most difficult position. This brave officer, always bold and dashing on the battlefield, had become distinctly moderate because he was convinced that the only hope of safety for France and for the Emperor lay in peace.

He argued his cause before Napoleon with admirable frankness, and we are safe in saying that if his prudent counsels had been followed, the Empire would have been saved. Among the Allies, especially the English and the Austrian, we believe that there was no ill-will towards the Emperor; only, they had decided not to grant better conditions than those which had been accorded the Bourbons. That is what Napoleon could never comprehend. To the last he imagined that his marriage would bring him sooner or later the sympathies of Austria, and he let himself be deluded by this expectation, which the Duke of Vicenza, more clear-sighted than his master, never shared for a moment.

It was a melancholy situation for this man who had filled the highest diplomatic posts at a period when France had been feared and admired, and now was forced to carry on negotiations grievous and humiliating. He had a hard position between the cruel demands of the Allies and the Emperor's obstinacy which rendered argument impossible. Caulaincourt was able to perform his difficult duties with nobility and dignity, and the study of the negotiations, which were thus made so laborious that no one else could have handled them at all, does the greatest honour to his intelligence and to his character. History, we are sure, will render justice to this excellent man.

The Allies showed so little eagerness for negotiating that the Duke of Vicenza waited for a month at the outposts for the conference to begin. It did not open till February 4, 1814, at Châtillon. The day before he had written to Marshal Berthier this letter:

> I write to Your Highness as the most devoted of the Emperor's servants. There has been another battle [that of 'Rothière] and the enemy have won another victory. Will not this stand in the way of our negotiations, make every question more difficult, and lead them to add to their demands?
>
> The evil genius that for three years has marred the happy destiny of the Emperor still haunts him. Has he not yet brought him sufficient misery? Tell the true state of things to His Majesty. Show him how serious matters are; that the slightest delay may imperil everything without bringing any advantage. Tell me plainly, Prince, have you an army? Can we discuss the conditions for a fortnight, or must we accept everything at once?
>
> If no one has the courage to tell me our real condition, I have no surer ground than the vague statements in M. de Bassano's gazette. It is with tales of that sort that we have lost all our conquests; and they will not help to save France. It is not my fault, for I am continually begging the Emperor to give me his orders, rather with a view of serving and satisfying him than of seeking to shun responsibility. In the name of our master, in the name of all you hold most dear, speak to him, Prince; write to me, and let us save the throne and the country!

The Emperor, who was then in a most critical position, made no explanation. He simply left the Duke of Vicenza free to act as he pleased, reserving the right to disavow him if he desired. Hence the Duke of Bassano wrote from Troyes to the French plenipotentiary, February 5, 1814:

> I have sent you a messenger with a letter of His Majesty and the renewal of the full powers which you asked for. When His Majesty was leaving this city, he charged me to send you this, and to tell you in so many words that His Majesty gives you *carte blanche* to conduct the negotiations to a happy end, to save the capital, and prevent a battle on which the last hopes of the nation shall depend.

On the receipt of this unexpected authorization, Caulaincourt wrote to the Emperor, February 6:

> I had started with my hands tied, and I receive unlimited powers. I was restrained, and now I am urged on. Yet I am not informed of the reasons for this change. In my ignorance of the real state of affairs, I cannot judge what it requires and what it permits: whether it is such that I ought to consent blindly to everything—and there is no room for discussion or delay—or whether to discuss at least the most essential points I have several days before me or only one, or whether I have not even a moment.

February 7, the plenipotentiaries of the Allies showed a rough draft of the demands of the Powers, demanding that France should return to the boundaries of 1792, and should have nothing to say about the fate of the countries to be ceded. What should be done with Poland, Saxony, Westphalia, Belgium, Italy, how Bavaria, Würtemberg, Switzerland, were to be treated, was not to concern France. Finally, an answer, yes or no, was demanded, before the conference should begin.

As Thiers says:

> Certainly Napoleon had misused victory; but even in the intoxication of Rivoli, of Austerlitz, of Jena, of Friedland, he had never treated the vanquished in that way.

Nevertheless, the Duke of Vicenza appeared inclined to accept these harsh terms, but on one condition: that he should be at least assured that by accepting them, he could at once stop the enemy, and thus save Paris and the Imperial throne. It was answered that there would be a suspension of hostilities only in case of their immediate unreserved acceptance, and only after the ratification of the treaty. The next day, February 8, it was announced that the conference was suspended.

Then the French plenipotentiary, in the deepest despair, wrote to Prince Metternich, who was with the Emperor of Austria, the following letter:

> Châtillon, February 8, 1814. You have given me leave, Prince, to express myself to you without reserve. I have already done so, and I shall continue to do so; it is a consolation which I should find it hard to deny myself. I regret more every day that it is not with you that I have to treat. If I could have foreseen this, I should not have accepted the appointment, I should not have been here. I should be with the army; and I could at least find in battle a death which I should count as a blessing, if I cannot serve here my sovereign and my country.
>
> Do the Allies wish to get time to reach Paris? I will not ask you, Prince, to think of the consequences to the Empress of such an event. Should she be compelled to flee before her father's troops, when her august husband is ready to sign a peace?
>
> But I will tell you that all France is not in Paris; that with the capital occupied, the French may think that the time for sacrifices is past; that feelings, now repressed for several reasons, may awaken, and that the arrival of the Allies at Paris may be the beginning of a series of events which Austria may not be the last to regret having overlooked. Now, ought we to end by being overwhelmed? Is it to the interest of Austria that we should be?
>
> What profit, what glory, can she expect if we succumb under the assaults of all Europe? You, my Prince, you have a chance to win vast glory, but on one condition, that you

remain in control of affairs; and your only way of securing your hold is by stopping their course by a speedy peace. We refuse no reasonable sacrifice. We only wish to know all that are asked of us, for whose advantage we are to make them, and whether, by making them, we can have the certainty of putting an end to the horrors of war. See to it, Prince, that all these questions are put in perfect sincerity. I shall not delay my answer.

You are assuredly too wise not to perceive that our demand is as just as our disposition is moderate. Cannot Your Excellency come with M. de Nesselrode and spend three hours here with Lord Castlereagh? It would well accord with the character of the Emperor of Austria, with the heart of the Empress's father, to consent to an expedition which might in a single morning terminate a struggle now without an object, and one that costs humanity so many tears!

After a week's interruptions, the meetings of the Congress were resumed, and Prince Metternich thus answered the letter of the Duke of Vicenza:

Troyes, February 15, 1814. We have just started the negotiations again, my dear Duke, and I can assure Your Excellency that it is not an easy thing to be the minister of the Coalition. All your kind words of regret at not seeing me at Châtillon can only spring from your personal feelings of which you have given me so many proofs. I have already recommended to you Count Stadion.

Take my word for it, Lord Castlereagh is also a man of the best sort, upright, loyal, without passion, and so without prejudice. It needs a combination of men like the English ministers of the present time to render possible the great task at which you are working, and which, I flatter myself, will be crowned with success. Your Excellency has no reason to regret accepting your position. It is a great one only in difficult times.

I enclose a letter from the Mesgrigny family to their brothers, sons, etc. Be good enough to forward it to them. They are excellent people who have the good fortune to have me in their house,—a real piece of good fortune, for I don't eat them. War, dear Duke, is a horrible thing, especially when it is waged with fifty thousand Cossacks and Baskirs

Certainly diplomatists have their own ways of writing, and this lively style was in marked contrast to the gravity of the events!

Meanwhile, Napoleon, who for a moment had thought that all was lost, had won the battles of Champaubert, Montmirail, and Vauchamps, and intoxicated by his success, had imagined himself nearer to Munich and Vienna than were the Allies to Paris. Then he wrote to Caulaincourt this letter:

Nangis, February 18. I gave you *carte blanche* to save Paris and avoid a battle, which was the nation's last hope. The battle has been fought; Providence has favoured our side. I have made thirty or forty thousand prisoners, have captured two hundred cannon, a great number of generals, and destroyed several armies almost without striking a blow. Yesterday I routed the army of Prince Schwarzenberg, which I hope to destroy before it has recrossed our frontier. Your attitude must remain the same; you must do everything to secure peace; but I desire that you sign nothing without my order, because I alone know how I stand.

No, General, I want only a solid and honourable peace, and that can only be on the bases proposed at Frankfort [*the natural frontiers*]. If the Allies had accepted your propositions on the 9th, there would have been no battle; I should not have run the risk at a moment when the slightest ill-success would have ruined France; in short, I should not have known the secret of their weakness. It is proper that I should have in return the advantages of the chances which have turned in my favour. I desire peace, but that would not be a peace which should impose on France more humiliating conditions than the Frankfort propositions.

My position is certainly more favourable than when the Allies were at Frankfort; they were able to defy me, I had obtained no advantage over them, and they were far from my territory. Today it is very different; I have won many victories over them, victories unequalled in a somewhat illustrious career of twenty years. I am ready to cease hostilities and to let the enemy withdraw unmolested if they will sign the preliminaries based on the Frankfort propositions.

Napoleon believed the Coalition much more shaken than it really was. At the meeting of February 17, the plenipotentiaries of the Allies presented a series of preliminary articles even more insulting than the previous drafts. It was simply stated that Germany would form a federation; that Holland would be enlarged by the addition of Belgium, and be made a kingdom; that Italy was to be independent of France; that Austria would have possessions there; and that France would return to the boundaries of 1792.

When Napoleon, who believed that he had scattered terror among his enemies, heard of their propositions, he was filled with wrath. He wrote from Surville to the Duke of Vicenza, February 19:

I am so deeply moved by the infamous proposition which you send to me, that I feel dishonoured by the mere fact that it was made to you. Everything they tell you is false. The Austrians are beaten in Italy, and far from being at Meaux, I shall soon be at Châtillon. I shall send you word of my intentions from Troyes or Châtillon; but I think I should have done better to lose Paris than to see such propositions made to the French people. You are always talking about the Bourbons. I had rather see the Bourbons in France, under reasonable conditions, than the infamous propositions which you send to me.

The same day, February 19, 1814, Caulaincourt, who was far from taking the same optimistic view of things, wrote to the Duke of Bassano:

> Thanks to your good news, I am full of hope. But let us not, from lack of proper moderation, lose the chance to make a peace which will be ever honourable, if it is truly reasonable. Delays or claims made now, when Europe is in such a state of exasperation with us, may ruin everything in a mome. Plead the cause of peace, Duke; it is that of the Emperor's real glory and of the real interest of France.

Caulaincourt did not yet wholly despair of a happy outcome of the negotiations; Lord Castlereagh, who, as the head of the English Cabinet, had come to Châtillon, though he took no part in the meetings of the Congress, while exercising a preponderant influence, had not yet displayed a systematic hostility to Napoleon personally. Hence the Duke of Vicenza wrote to the Duke of Bassano, February 21:

> In general, the way the English express themselves, their tone, and the moderation of Lord Castlereagh's opinions, the very proper way in which they speak of the Emperor and of France, have been really remarkable. I owe it to the truth to render them this justice.

The plenipotentiaries of the Allies, while polite in externals, were pitiless in fact. February 28, they informed the Duke of Vicenza that they granted him a delay of ten days for his answer to their proposition of February 17; that they were ready to discuss any modifications that France might suggest, but that they would absolutely refuse any which should depart in the least from the essential points of the proposition. It was agreed that if this delay of ten days, expiring March 10, should pass without their coming to an understanding, the Congress should be at once dissolved.

At the same time, Lord Castlereagh was the promoter of the famous agreement which was the germ of the Holy Alliance. March 1, 1814, England, Austria, Prussia, and Russia agreed, by the treaty of Chaumont, to furnish each a permanent contingent of one hundred and fifty thousand men until the war should be ended. England offered in addition an annual subsidy of one hundred and fifty million *francs*, to be divided equally between Russia, Prussia, and Austria. Lord Castlereagh did not stop there. He bound the four Powers for twenty years from the next peace. They were each, when the war was over, to maintain sixty thousand men for twenty years, for the use of that one of them which France might try to attack, if, after peace was once made, she should renew her assaults against her neighbours.

Caulaincourt was not informed of the treaty of Chaumont, but he perceived that the Allies were forming serious resolutions, and, March 3, he wrote a private letter to the Emperor, expressing his uneasiness; it ran as follows:—

Sire: The details which I have to report to Your Majesty seeming to me alarming, I make them the subject of a private letter. May this report be received with less bitterness than those I usually have the honour of sending to Your Majesty, and prove to him that his plenipotentiary has the most thorough conviction of the dangers of the throne when he ventures to recur to questions and sacrifices which he knows are equally painful.

Your Majesty has not been ignorant that the princes of the house of Bourbon who have left England were established on our frontiers, and that the Count d'Artois, who was just now in Switzerland, has settled at Vesoul. Today he is said to be even nearer the enemy's headquarters. This Prince was able to come to Switzerland without the consent of all the Allies, but he could not come into France or stay on the line mainly occupied by the Austrian forces save with the consent of Your Majesty's father-in-law. Hence his presence is more than a Russian and English menace. Your Majesty is more competent than anyone to draw all the consequences from this apparition under such a flag. It is, I shall be told, a mere bugbear, an empty threat. The present generation has no knowledge of the Bourbons, and consequently takes no interest in them; old people have forgotten them, and the people of La Vendée, if they remember their courageous efforts in behalf of these princes, have not lost the memory of their abandonment and of their stay at Île Dieu.

I know and think of all that, Sire; I know too that the inhabitants of La Vendée owe to you the reconstruction of their manors and the present prosperity of their country. Hence I should not ascribe excessive importance to this resurrection if I did not infer that Austria, being void of shame for such conduct, is ready to disown us. In this state of affairs it is the duty of the man placed by Your Majesty as his first political sentinel to call all your attention to the consequence of this appearance.

You should believe me when I return to this grave matter; for you know that no interest, no passion, moves me against the Bourbons, since, the Revolution having made me its victim and then a soldier, it is not it, but my own sword and my Emperor, that have made me what I am. You know too that the memories of my infancy and my respect for misfortune do not make me dream of these princes, since, in my opinion, the interest and the glory of my country oppose them now, as well as our oath to our Emperor. I hope, then, that these reflections will give weight to my urgency, which comes from my profound conviction.

In the same letter the Duke of Vicenza reported an important conversation which he had just had with an intimate friend of. Prince Metternich:

Prince Esterhazy, whose relations with Prince Metternich are well known to Your Majesty, and who has been with him since the beginning of the campaign, has just passed a few moments here. These are the remarks of his to which I paid particular attention: 'It is the personal opinion of Emperor Francis and of Metternich that peace is more and more imperatively necessary for France. If it is delayed, it is impossible to foresee how far things will go, for defeats would add to the exasperation of the Allies as much as would success. Your vast ambition and a thousand circumstances have produced the present crisis and summoned all Europe to arms.

In the present state of Europe, millions of men will march if the eight hundred thousand now blocking every road to Paris are not enough. It is too clear that your sovereign, deceiving himself with the vain hope of restoring his condition by gaining a battle, stakes on this single card not only the existence of France, but his throne, and even his life.

Why push things to the bitter end, when we cannot conceal the fact that everyone has more than one insult to avenge? Had it not been for Austria, the Allies would already have lost some of the regard for France, which cannot last long if we postpone the signing of a peace; for in the present war Austria alone is without passion. Emperor Francis loves his daughter and takes a real interest in his son-in-law; why reject his good advice? Before long his good intentions and those of Prince Metternich will be unable further to control passions inflamed by the prolongation of the struggle.

Is there then no way of enlightening the Emperor Napoleon about his position and of saving him, if he insists on ruining himself; and has he absolutely placed his own fate, that of his son, your own, on his last cannon? Would you rather have France pillaged and the Russians in Paris than treat for peace? Will all your audacity and the courage of despair prevent your being overwhelmed by the multitude that threatens you? Believe me, make peace. We are enemies—you know it better than anyone, for your sovereign has confided to you the conditions of peace—only because the Emperor Napoleon has made us such.

After thus recording the words of Prince Esterhazy, the Duke of Vicenza closed his letter with these words:

Your Majesty can no longer hide from himself that what was possible at Frankfort is impossible at Châtillon. The enemy have tested the national and patriotic resistance which they feared, and they are, besides, in force at the gates of Paris. Doubtless these are not consoling reflections, and it is hard for me to address such language to Your Majesty; but I owe to you absolute truthfulness. Austria and Prussia, when conquered by you, gave you for saving themselves more than one example of resignation; this virtue has been of service to those cabinets, since now they speak as conquerors. Imitate them, Sire, while your capital is still uninvaded and victory has not yet deserted you. Your Majesty can no longer deceive yourself. You see that our ranks are too empty to triumph over so many foes. You have learned that your fortune has been able to save nothing but our laurels. Hence you have had it proved that we must await from the future what the present denies us, and that only on this condition can the hour of a noble and glorious vengeance ever strike.

The Duke of Vicenza, fully appreciating the remarks of Prince Esterhazy, went on:

Does Prince Esterhazy's conduct have any connection with the appearance of the Bourbons? He said nothing to me bearing upon them, and in speaking of them I took care not to admit that Your Majesty could have any uneasiness in this regard. Does it have any connection with other circumstances or with arrangements now unknown to us? Time alone can tell. We may presume everything when we have everything to fear. By what he called 'regard for France,' etc., may he not have understood a plan to admit the Bourbons in the case the war is prolonged? Everything that occurs, everything said, everything that threatens us, shows that our foes regard all means as lawful.

Despite this state of affairs, I, like Your Majesty, would take counsel only of my courage, if I knew that you had in your hands one hundred and twenty thousand men to face the storm; but if, as I fear, you have less than eighty thousand, but one thing is left to do,—to yield at this moment to united Europe; for peace, I repeat, has become the desire and necessity of the French; there is no safety but in peace. Our dangers are too real, and the hours left us are, it is clear, counted by our relentless enemies. Possibly Your Majesty will charge these reflections with weakness; I think, however, and it cannot escape you, that courage is required to make them. However, I am convinced that the time is come when no consideration should stop me.

It is almost impossible to tell the truth to sovereigns in the days of their prosperity; it is not easy to make them listen to it when adversity has given them lessons by which they should profit. This frank and loyal letter of Caulaincourt's displeased the Emperor. On hearing of this unreasonable displeasure, the faithful servant wrote to Napoleon this admirable letter:—

Châtillon, March 5, 1814. Sire: I must state clearly to Your Majesty how much I am pained by finding my devotion misunderstood. You are dissatisfied with me; you show this, and you charged M. de Rumigny to tell me. My frankness has displeased you; and you call it rudeness and harshness. You reproach me with seeing the Bourbons everywhere, and yet, perhaps wrongly, I scarcely mentioned them. Your Majesty forgets that it is you who first spoke of them in letters written or dictated to me.

To foresee, like you, the chances that may be offered to them by the passions of some of the Allies, those that might be produced by an unhappy contingency, and by the interest with which their sufferings might inspire this country, if the presence of a Prince and a party should arouse this old memory at a critical moment, would not be so unreasonable, if things were pushed to an extreme. In the present condition of men's minds, in this feverish state of Europe, when France is so anxious and fatigued, every possibility should be faced; wisdom commands this. I well understand that Your Majesty should desire to communicate the force of his nature, the fire of his great character to all who serve him, and to inspire every one with his energy. But your minister, Sire, does not need this spur. Adversity arouses his courage instead of casting it down.

No one would more readily than I console Your Majesty, soften all the pain that the circumstances and the necessary sacrifices inflict upon you, but the interest of France, that of your dynasty, command me to be above all things cautious and honest.

Is it my fault if I am the only one to use this language of devotion to Your Majesty, if those who are with you and agree with me dread to displease you, and, desirous of sparing you amid so many trials, dare not say what it is my duty to tell you?

The conclusion of this letter is both noble and touching. It is easy to see all the anguish that rent Caulaineourt's heart when he wrote these lines.

What glory, what advantage, could there be for me in signing this same peace, if it should ever be made? Will not this peace, or rather these sacrifices, ever be for Your Majesty a source of lasting dissatisfaction with your plenipotentiary? Will not many Frenchmen who now feel its necessity blame me for it six months after it shall have saved your throne?

Since I am no blinder about my position than I am about Your Majesty's, you ought to believe me. I see things as they are. Fear has united all the sovereigns, discontent has collected all the Germans; the bond is too strong for us to break. In accepting the ministry as I did, in undertaking this negotiation, I devoted myself to your service, to save my country. I had no other aim, and that would seem to me high and noble enough to be above all sacrifices. In my position I could not do otherwise, and that is what decided me. Your Majesty may say of me all the ill you please; you cannot think it in your heart, and you will be forced always to do me the justice of regarding me as one of your most faithful subjects and one of the best citizens of this France which I cannot be suspected of wishing to degrade, since I would give my life to save one of its villages.

Meanwhile, the fatal limit set by the plenipotentiaries of the Coalition, the 10th of March, had come. On that day the Duke of Vicenza handed in a statement referring to the protocol, and recalling what the different states had gained since 1792. He expressed himself as follows:

After demanding so many sacrifices of France, but one was left to claim,—that of its honour. The proposal tends to deprive her of the right of intervening in favour of one of her former unhappy allies. The plenipotentiary of France having asked whether the King of Saxony was to be put again in possession of his states, could not get an answer. From France are demanded cessions and renunciations, and it is desired that she should make these cessions without knowing to whom, by what title, and in what proportions, will belong what she shall have ceded.

It is intended that she shall not know who will be her nearest neighbours. It is desired to arrange, without her, the fate of countries she shall have renounced, and the way of living of those with which her sovereign was bound by close ties. It is desired without her, to make arrangements determining the general system of European equilibrium. It is desired that she should have no part in the arrangement of a whole of which she forms a considerable and necessary part. It is, moreover, desired that by subscribing to these conditions she should be in some sort excluded from European society.

Attacked at once by all the Powers united against her, the French nation, more than any other, needs peace, and desires it more than any other; but every people, like every generous man, sets honour even above life.

After hearing this statement, the plenipotentiaries broke out into the most violent abuse. Where, they asked, is the counter-project which has been expected for a month and had been solemnly promised for March 10? The Duke of Vicenza succeeded only with great difficulty in calming them and in obtaining a few days' respite. At last, March 15, he handed in the counter-project, which was Napoleon's own work. Therein the Emperor agreed to cede the Dutch Brabant and various parcels of territory on the right bank of the Rhine, but he demanded a sum of money for Prince Eugene, another for Princess Elisa, and kept the Rhine, and the Alps, Antwerp, Cologne, Mayence, Chambéry, Nice. The allied plenipotentiaries regarded this counter-project as an insulting defiance.

Then Prince Metternich wrote to the Duke of Vicenza a final private letter, in which he said:

If the conditions of the counter-project are the Emperor Napoleon's ultimatum, peace is impossible, and the fate of France and of Europe will be decided by arms. It would be hard, Duke, to describe to you all the painful emotions of the Emperor, my master. He loves his daughter, and he sees her exposed to new anxieties which can only increase. The more complicated the political questions, the more personal they become. The Emperor Napoleon has not seconded the favourable intentions which the Emperor Francis has always manifested. Possibly we are nearer peace by the breaking off of these futile negotiations. That is the sole object of our prayers.

March 18, the plenipotentiaries of the Allies read a formal

note in which they stated that, France having exactly reproduced all the conditions recognized as inacceptable by Europe,
the conferences were definitely broken off. Yet a final note was
exchanged the next day, March 19; it was about the Pope. It ran
thus:

The undersigned, the plenipotentiaries of the allied courts,
seeing with a deep and profound regret the fruitlessness of
the negotiation undertaken at Châtillon for the tranquillity of Europe, cannot dispense with occupying themselves
before their departure, by means of the present note to
His Excellency, the French Plenipotentiary, with a subject
which is foreign to political dissensions, and which should
always have remained so. In insisting on the independence
of Italy, the allied Powers had intended to replace the Holy
Father in his former capital. The French government has
shown the same disposition in the counter-project presented by its plenipotentiary.
It would be unfortunate if so just and natural a design,
agreed to by the two parties, were to remain without effect through reasons in no way concerning the functions
which the Head of the Catholic Church is religiously
bound to perform. The religion professed by a great part
of the nations now at war—justice and general equity, humanity; in a word—are equally interested in setting His
Holiness at liberty, and the undersigned are convinced that
they have only to express this wish, and in the name of
the courts to ask this act of justice of the French government, to engage it to put the Holy Father in a condition
to satisfy the needs of the Catholic Church, by the enjoy-
ment of perfect liberty. The undersigned avail themselves
of this opportunity to reassure His Excellency, the French
Plenipotentiary, of their high consideration. [Signed.]
Count Stadion, Count Rasumowski, Cathcart, Humboldt,
Charles Stuart, Aberdeen.

The Duke of Vicenza answered this note thus:

The undersigned, Plenipotentiary of France, will be the more glad to transmit to his court the note, dated today, of Their Excellencies, the allied plenipotentiaries, since the Emperor, his master, in the counter-project which he was charged with presenting on the 15th, has first shown the interest he took in the Holy Father.

Thus ended the Congress of Châtillon. Of the four allied Powers, only one, Austria, is Roman Catholic; and at the last moment when the negotiations on all other points are broken off, they occupy themselves with the Holy See. And the French plenipotentiary pays homage to Napoleon's prisoner. That was the last word of the Congress, which failed so disastrously for the Empire! In a few days the Emperor, at the end of his resources, exhausted, betrayed by fortune, was to reappear at Fontainebleau in the apartment next to the one that served as the prison of Pius VII. Nothing is more impressive than these unexpected changes in history. In this curious interweaving of events, outdoing human calculations, we see new proof of the maxim:

Man proposes; God disposes.

March 19, the Duke of Vicenza withdrew from the other plenipotentiaries, and, on the 20th, all the legations left Châtillon to return to the headquarters of the different armies. These useless protocols, these vain diplomatic debates, as they are recorded in the volumes in the Ministry of Foreign Affairs, entitled "The Châtillon Congress," are melancholy reading. Let us turn to the military operations where we left off at the beginning of the second fortnight of March, 1814.

6

Arcis-Sur-Aube

At the beginning of the second fortnight of March, 1814, Napoleon did not yet despair. On reaching Rheims on the 14th, he found that warlike and patriotic city illuminated and echoing with cries of "Long live the Emperor!" He stayed there three days, directing the complicated affairs of his Empire with imperturbable calm and untiring activity. Meanwhile Blücher, at the head of the army of Silesia, was resting quietly on the hill of Laon, and Schwarzenberg, although victorious over the Duke of Reggio, seemed chained to Troyes. Napoleon, ever confident in his fortune, in spite of so many disasters, awaited some misstep on the part of his adversaries, to fall upon them with the swiftness of lightning. For him it was of the utmost importance to prevent the junction of the armies of Silesia and of Bohemia, and to strike a strong blow upon Schwarzenberg's forces while the two armies were still separate.

The Emperor determined to attack the enemy in spite of their numerical superiority. He ordered Marmont and Mortier, with their eighteen thousand men, to oppose Blücher's march to Paris with a hundred and twenty thousand men, and he himself, with about seventeen thousand, advanced against Schwarzenberg's one hundred thousand. Thus a handful of soldiers, recruits wasted by suffering, or scanty veterans in the empty and disorganized ranks, were about to hurl themselves with the courage of heroes against the formidable army of Bohemia.

This fearless attacking column, led by Napoleon, started from

Rheims, March 17, and reached Épernay the same day: then the Emperor received bad news; namely, that the English had entered Bordeaux by the invitation of the mayor. March 19, the army advanced over the bridge of Plancy, by the ford of Charny, over the two arms of the Aube, through the space between the Aube and the Seine, and crossed the Seine itself. The highway between Troyes and Paris was in their hands, and the enemy knew a moment of terror.

The tidings of Napoleon's return to the Seine disconcerted the leaders of the Coalition. The main headquarters of the Allies were withdrawn to Troyes, and the heavy baggage was sent still further back; and a retreat to Bar was proposed. The Emperor Alexander was so anxious that he himself said that half of his hair would turn gray. This alarm, however, was of but brief duration. The Czar decided that instead of retreating, the armies of Silesia and of Bohemia ought to unite in the plains of Châlons. Consequently Blücher drew near to the banks of the Marne, and Schwarzenberg moved on Arcis; there it was that Napoleon, under the impression that he had to face an isolated army corps, was about to meet the whole army of Bohemia.'

The battle of Arcis-sur-Aube, which was fought March 20, 1814, and continued the next day, was the last battle but one that Napoleon fought; the very last being "Waterloo. Never was the Emperor in greater peril. For the first time, perhaps, since that terrible campaign had begun, he was overwhelmed by despair and anxious to die. When the enemy were on the point of surrounding him, he tried to draw his sword, but it had rusted in its scabbard, and it required the strength of his two equerries, Foulers and Saint Aignan, to get it out.

At the same moment, a shell fell before a battalion of conscripts, who were not yet used to the sight, and Napoleon rode his horse over the shell to teach them to despise danger, and doubtless, too, to die the death of a hero. Excelmans tried to stop him. "Let him go," shouted Sébastiani; "you see he does it on purpose: he wants to end it all." Napoleon wanted death, but death did not want him. The shell exploded, and for a moment he was lost to sight in a cloud of flame and smoke, but he came forth safe and sound: only his horse had been hit. The young soldiers, amazed at the Emperor's boldness, applauded him, and broke into cheers when he got on another horse.

His danger, however, only grew greater instead of less; a band of Russian and Bavarian cavalry renewed their charge. It seemed certain that Napoleon, who was defended by a mere handful of men, would be taken prisoner. General Drouot saved him: he saw a battery abandoned in the rout, rallied the artillerymen, aimed the pieces himself, and firing into the mingled mass of the French and the enemy, finally cleared the ground: then the Emperor charged at the head of the four squadrons of his body-guard, and drove away their threatening assailants.

In this way was the third birthday of the King of Rome celebrated. How vast the difference between the Tuileries of 1811 and this battle-field of 1814, between the salvos of artillery announcing the birth of an heir to this immense Empire and roar of cannon in this last battle but one, when the desperate warrior vainly sought death! Napoleon was often to regret that he had been spared by shell and bullet at Arcis-sur-Aube, and remembered this when, a few weeks later, at Fontainebleau, after his abdication, he vainly attempted to poison himself.

The battle of Arcis forms an heroic page in the Emperor's history: twenty thousand Frenchmen had held their ground against a body which was enlarged from forty thousand to ninety thousand men. When night came, the French army gathered under the walls of the houses in the suburbs, and the artillery duel continued. The castle of M. de la Briffe, the Emperor's headquarters, was thoroughly riddled by the cannon-balls.

The next morning Napoleon was averse to retreating, and refused to believe in the great numerical superiority of the enemy; when he was convinced by the evidence, after lashing the ground with his riding-whip, which he always did in moments of great excitement, he sacrificed his pride and commanded a retreat. There being but one bridge over the Aube, he had another built, and after keeping his troops deployed in front of Arcis while the second bridge was building, he suddenly withdrew them through the streets of the town, and following them across the Aube, had both bridges destroyed. Prince Schwarzenberg, furious at seeing his prey escape, tried in vain to cross the river. This was on the part of the French a retreat, though an heroic retreat.

Twice in ten days had the great general, so long invincible, been compelled to retreat: at Laon, before the army of Silesia; at Arcis, before the army of Bohemia. His prestige was lost; what more could he do? It was no longer possible to fight against either one of the two armies; how would it be when they had combined? Would he have to bow his head and humbly beg for the frontier of 1792? The untiring hero never fancied for a moment that the time had come to yield. He devised a new plan, and determined to march towards the east, in the hope of uniting the garrisons in the fortresses and the armed peasants in the outlying departments, of cutting the communications of the Allies, and thus compelling them to suspend their march on Paris.

Napoleon did not delay the execution of this new plan, which was bolder than anything he had yet done. March 21, he had just abandoned Arcis and crossed the Aube; when he had got out of the pass, beyond Ormes, accompanied only by his equerry, Baron de Saint Aignan, he stopped and asked for his field-glass; this he rested on the equerry's shoulder, while he examined the enemy's army. Then he remounted his horse and rode slowly and silently along the highroad.

"His revery became so profound," says General de Ségur, "that his hands dropped the reins and hung motionless by his side. He happened at the time to be ascending a steep path alongside of a precipice, down which the least misstep might have thrown him. Saint Aignan, not stopping to choose his words in his eagerness, warned him that there was no railing: he barely heard him; doubtless at that moment he was deciding on one of those important steps which are great or foolish, according to the event."

Meanwhile, Marie Louise still deceived herself about the

condition of France, and refused to believe that diplomatic negotiations were permanently broken off. Under this impression, she wrote to her father, March 22, a letter, in which she said:

The nation is full of courage and energy, the peasants are particularly aroused by the bad treatment they have received. Your troops may very probably be beaten. The Emperor's armies are finer and stronger than ever. It is for your interest as well as ours to propose anew the Frankfort conditions. Otherwise you may be compelled to make a less favourable peace in a few months.

The letter ended with these entreaties:

In the name of all you hold most sacred, I beg of you, do not let yourself be carried away by the greed of the English, by the ambition and hatred of Count Stadion. If you do, you will sacrifice the interest of your Empire, the happiness of your family, and your own peace of mind. The humiliating peace proposed to us it is impossible to accept. You may be sure that I know the Emperor and that he will never agree to it. You ought to return to the Frankfort conditions, the only ones advantageous to France and Austria.

This appeal was made to deaf ears. The Allies, fired by their last victories, determined on destroying Napoleon. While Schwarzenberg, at the head of the army of Bohemia, forced the passage of the Aube at Arcis, Blücher, with the army of Silesia, reached the banks of the Marne by way of Rheims. He had driven back towards Château Thierry the corps of the Duke of Ragusa and the Duke of Treviso. March 23, the scouts of the army of Silesia and of the army of Bohemia met at Poivre. A great cry of joy arose when these two great invading armies came in sight of each other.

Never, since the time of Attila had more soldiers been assembled on the vast plain between Châlons and Arcis-sur-Aube. Two hundred thousand allies, in a compact body, separated the thirty-six or forty thousand worn-out soldiers of Napoleon, on his way to Lorraine, from the twenty-thousand men of Marmont, Mortier, and Pacthod, scattered between Vertus and Sézanne. The evening of March 23, the Allies issued a proclamation announcing to France the breaking off of the negotiations of Châtillon. The last scene of the military drama was approaching.

7

The March to the East

With such vast forces facing him, Napoleon was unable to move in the direction of his capital; hence he conceived another, bolder plan, which might have been successful if there had been no traitors in France. He resolved to march eastward, and cut the base of the enemy's operations. In three days he could be at Metz, and there he could unite the garrisons of that city, of Mayence, Luxembourg, Thionville, Verdun, Strassburg, amounting to thirty thousand men, await a re-enforcement of fifteen thousand from the Low Countries, and thus soon be at the head of an army of one hundred thousand combatants. He hoped, moreover, that Marshal Suchet, who had been sent to take Augereau's place in command of the army of Lyons, would be able to move to Besançon with forty thousand men, and that thus the face of things would be entirely changed.

But while fearless youths and courageous veterans did prodigies of valour to save the glory of France, there were men who did not blush to become the auxiliaries and accomplices of the foreigners. They were not the men of whom Napoleon had asked the greatest sacrifices without paying them with promotion, with office, or with money, and who had shown their devotion by tireless effort. No; they were the men whom he loaded with gold, with titles, with rewards of every sort, and who addressed him with the rankest flattery, and had times without number taken oaths of eternal fidelity. In the brilliant mansions which they owed to his generosity they formed their treacherous plans.

France, if it had not been divided against itself, might have triumphed over all its enemies; but it was divided into two hostile camps,—the Royalist and the Imperialist. There were men hastening to join the white flag of the Bourbons with the foreign flags, and eager to welcome the Cossacks on the boulevards as liberators. In the presence of such sentiments Napoleon's plans necessarily fell to the ground. It is easy to conceive the thoughts of the patriotic soldiers who had struggled so bravely against unheard of difficulties. When they saw a handful of traitors overthrowing the whole glorious edifice, and that they were the victims of their fellow-countrymen rather than of the foreigners, that all their heroic efforts and generous bloodshed had been thrown away, they exclaimed, "We have not been conquered; we have been betrayed!" Their cry of grief and wrath will echo from one age to another as the sublime protest of honour and loyalty!

The enemy hesitated on hearing of Napoleon's eastward march.

"They were not ignorant," says M. de Beauchamp, in his *History of the Campaign of 1814,* "that secret and full instructions had reached the garrison of the frontiers on the Rhine and the Moselle, to march forth at a given signal, and to join the army to be sent into Lorraine. But what required the most serious attention was the disposition shown by a great many of the peasants of Lorraine, Champagne, Alsace, Franche-Comté and Burgundy, who it appeared were ready to rise at the slightest defeat, to cut the bridges and destroy the roads, to burn the supplies, to annoy and starve out the enemy; in a word, to change the war into a national uprising, in answer to Napoleon's efforts."

An eye-witness who is above suspicion is Mr. Robert Wilson, an Englishman, from whom we quote:

"The Allies," he says, speaking of the campaign of 1814,

"were in a vicious circle, from which their only escape was the treachery of some of the French. They could not keep open the line of retreat, and yet retreat seemed unavoidable. This treachery that favoured them, and had been carefully prepared, came into effect at the very moment when Napoleon's success seemed assured; and his movement towards Saint Dizier, which should have secured the safety of his Empire, lost him his crown."

Who were the Frenchmen whose treachery thus aided the foreigners? Let us listen to one of them, the Abbé de Pradt, Archbishop of Mechlin, one of Napoleon's most prominent courtiers, a man whom he had loaded with benefits. In his account of the Restoration, he says:

The Allies, thus occupying a new position amid unfamiliar surroundings, were anxious to depend on the information of people whom they supposed more familiar with the internal condition of France. M. de Talleyrand and M. de Dalberg had especially attracted their attention. Though I had but few claims to this honour, it had yet been accorded me. Even our future had been provided for, in case it had been compromised by events. Our meetings with the persons mentioned above continued: sometimes they were frequent in one day.

The Châtillon Congress was our bane. Not a day passed without our undermining and destroying the Emperor's power, without our hastening the day of his fall. The French armies lay between Paris and the Allies, and it was with the greatest difficulty that we maintained communication with them. The first one to triumph over the obstacles was M. de Vitrolles, and it was through him that the ministers of the great Powers began to receive positive information about the condition of internal affairs, of which they had been in utter ignorance.

M. de Vitrolles was a baron of the Empire, an Imperial official, a postal agent. M. de Lavalette, his superior, did not in the least suspect him, and entrusted him with the arrangement of regular communications with Italy, by passage through Switzerland and the rear of the enemy's army. M. de Vitrolles pretended to accept this mission, but really went to the headquarters of the Allies, and then to the Count d'Artois.

As for M. de Talleyrand, whom the Emperor had made Minister of Foreign Affairs, Prince of Benevento, a high dignitary of the Empire, who to all appearance was the humble servant and attentive courtier of the Regent, he too conspired, but very prudently; for he desired to overthrow the Empire without himself running the slightest risk. While he was secretly weaving his Royalist plots, he made a great show of friendship for the Duke of Rovigo, the Minister of Police, and pretended to be very zealous in informing him of the plots and intrigues of the Count d'Artois.

The Duke of Rovigo suspected double dealing, but he did not feel sure.

"I was riding," he says in his *Memoirs*, "when it occurred to me to pass by the house of Prince Talleyrand. I saw the carriage of the Archbishop of Mechlin at his door. I fancied that they were in conference. Being anxious to make sure, instead of riding into the courtyard, I alighted in the street, and entered swiftly on foot. The janitor knew me and did not dare to stop me. I hastily ascended the staircase and reached M. de Talleyrand's private room without meeting any one; he was alone with the Archbishop. My sudden entrance startled them as much as if I had come in through the window. The conversation, which had been animated, stopped short; they were both struck dumb. The face of the Archbishop especially expressed great agitation.

Their confusion suggested to me the subject of their talk, and I could not keep from saying: 'This time you won't deny it; I have caught you conspiring.' I had guessed right. They began to laugh and tried to make some reply; but it was in vain that I asked them to resume their, conversation: they could not. I withdrew, convinced that they were weaving some plot, but what it was I did not know."

In the *Memorial of Saint Selena* we read:

When about to leave the Tuileries, Napoleon, who already expected treason, determined to seize the man who in fact turned out to be the soul of the conspiracy that overthrew him. He was only prevented by the assurances, and we might almost say the almost personal guarantee, of some of the ministers, who proved to him that the one suspected was the very man whom the Bourbons most feared.

These, ministers were mistaken. As Thiers has said: "Some insinuations of persons in relation with the Bourbons had informed M. de Talleyrand, what in fact he already knew, that the services of a married bishop would be very well received by the most pious princes, for there is nothing which is not forgotten in the face of services not rendered, but to be rendered. Parties have memories only for what they please; according to their necessities, they forget everything or remember everything." There is much truth" in this last statement of the historian.

When the treason was once organized, secret emissaries were despatched to the enemy's camp. "You have the game in your hands, and yet hold back; be bold!" They added: "Paris detests its tyrant, and only your presence is needed for proclamation to be made of his deposition and for the Bourbons to be summoned." Still the Allies hesitated, when, in the night of March 23, Emperor Alexander and Prince Schwarzenberg, who were staying at the castle of Dampierre, received information of two letters that had been intercepted, one from Marie Louise, the other from the Duke of Rovigo, both addressed to Napoleon. These two letters proved the existence in Paris of a party in league with the foreigners.

When he had read these letters, the Czar decided that the march on Paris should begin at sunrise the next morning. He left Dampierre early the next day, the 24th, and met the King of

Prussia and Blücher at Sompuis. The allied armies then started, the army of Silesia on the right, that of Bohemia on the left, for Fère-Champenoise, moving towards the capital between the Marne and the Seine. The Emperor of Russia and the King of Prussia marched with their troops. As for the Emperor of Austria, who was less eager than his allies, he was then at Bar-sur-Aube, and he was advised not to join the invading column, lest he should fall into the hands of his son-in-law; and he was persuaded to return to Dijon, that he might be spared the dethronement of his own daughter.

Meanwhile, Napoleon was continuing his march eastward. March 21, he had spent the night at Sompuis; the 22nd, he crossed the Marne at the ford of Frignicourt; the 23rd, he slept at Saint Dizier, where he was met by the Duke of Vicenza returning from the Châtillon Congress.

"You did well to return," the Emperor said to him; "for I will tell you frankly, if you had accepted the ultimatum of the Allies, I should have disavowed you. This time it shall not be said that I am fighting for my ambition, for it would be easy to save my throne; but my throne, with France humiliated, is not what I want. You are going to see some great things. I am going to march on the fortified towns, and assemble thirty or forty thousand men in a few days. Evidently the enemy are following me. There is no other explanation of the mass of cavalry surrounding us. My sudden appearance on their rear has brought Schwarzenberg back, and he will not dare to move on Paris while I am threatening his communications. Soon I shall have a hundred thousand men; then I shall fall on whichever is nearer, Blücher or Schwarzenberg. I shall crush him, and the peasants of Burgundy will finish him. The Coalition is nearer its own ruin than mine; and if I triumph, we shall tear up those abominable treaties. If I am mistaken, well, we shall die; we shall do what so many of our old companions in arms do every day; but we shall at least die with our honour untainted."

Napoleon was full of enthusiasm, and had genuine confidence in the success of the bold plan he had formed. His generals, however, did not have the same faith. In the next room they were muttering: "Where are we going? What will become of us? If he falls, shall we fall with him?" "As soon as the Emperor appeared, every one kept a respectful silence. "Yet," says General de Ségur, "he felt very clearly that the bravest were astonished, that human strength could do no more, that everything was exhausted. But his grandeur held itself aloof from these murmurs; he was still beyond their reach; such was the habit of command on his side, of obedience on theirs. Yet they respected his misfortune, and respected themselves in his presence; and whatever their despondency behind his back, they concealed it from him."

March 24, Napoleon marched to Joinville; the 25th, he pushed on his light cavalry to Chaumont. He fancied that he was pursued by the whole of Schwarzenberg's army, while in fact he had behind him only a few thousand of Witzingerode's cavalry; and he imagined Paris relieved at the very moment it was about to fall.

Mortier and Marmont had been attacked on the Aisne, the moment the Emperor. left them, and had been forced to evacuate Rheims, in order to cover the capital. But at Fère-Champenoise, March 25, they fell in with the whole army of Bohemia, and fought most bravely, though outnumbered ten to one. They were only saved from annihilation by Pacthod's division, which had been marching for four days to join them. This division, which had been made immortal by its courage, consisted entirely of National Guards. Its general exclaimed:

There is no surrender in the open field. Military law, and, above all, honour, forbids it. Besides, when the country is lost, who wishes to survive it? Let us then swear to die for it!

And they all swore it.

March 27, Napoleon heard of the disaster of Fère-Champenoise by a bulletin found on a prisoner. When he heard that the troops of Marmont and Mortier were routed, and that the Allies were moving on Paris, flushed with victory, he was most sorely perplexed. Macdonald urged him to pursue his movement eastward without concerning himself about Paris. "Let me consider," said the Emperor. "I must be alone."

His thoughts were most bitter. He, the most audacious of men, for the first time in his life was outdone in audacity by his adversaries. What was to become of Paris? Was not a revolution there imminent? And if Louis XVIII. were proclaimed in the capital, what would he, Napoleon, be in the departments of the east? The commander of an Imperial Vendée, a sort of adventurer or leader of a band. The whole night of the 27th he spent at Saint Dizier, poring over his maps, eagerly measuring the distances. Which was the shortest road to Paris? That of Cézanne to Coulommiers. But that road led to the Marne, and all the passages were guarded by the enemy. It would be better to take the road through Troyes, although it was far from straight.

Napoleon hesitated no longer; Paris became his sole objective point. But would he arrive in time? Would he not find the capital in possession of the Royalists and the Allies? With feverish impatience the Emperor gave the preparatory orders, and March 28, he set his troops in motion, starting from Saint Dizier; he spent that night at Doulevent. There he received a messenger from M. de Lavalette, the bearer of a letter running thus: "The friends of the foreigners, encouraged by what is going on at Bordeaux, are raising their heads; they are aided by secret plots. The presence of Napoleon is necessary if he wishes to prevent the surrender of the capital to the enemy. Not a moment must be lost."

March 29, the Emperor was again on horseback before day. Towards two in the afternoon he reached at the bridge of Doulancourt, the highroad of Troyes, whence he could advance either on Paris or on Lorraine. He hesitated for a moment. The wisest of his officers wanted to continue the march to the east, and their despair was great when they saw Napoleon, abandoning this plan, cross the Aube and take the road to Troyes, commanding his troops to follow him toward Paris, at double quick, night and day.

We read in the *Memorial of Saint Selena:*

> The Emperor much regretted that at Saint Dizier and at Doulevent he had yielded to the many arguments that urged him against his will to return to Paris. 'I lacked firmness,' he said. 'I ought steadily to have earned out my plan of advancing to the Rhine, strengthening myself with all my garrisons, putting myself at the head of the insurgent populace: I should have had an immense army. Murat would have returned to me at once; he and the Viceroy would have given me Vienna if the Allies had dared to take Paris. But no; the enemy would have shuddered at the dangers they were in, and the Allied sovereigns would have regarded as a favour the chance to retreat.'

The die was cast, and Napoleon had chosen the other course. He commanded General Dejean to leave at full speed to announce to the Parisians his return. The troops marched with wonderful celerity. The Imperial Guard and the baggage-train made fifteen leagues in a single day. March 29, Napoleon slept at Troyes. He was off again the morning of the 30th, and advanced as far as Villeneuve-l'Archevêque, where he stopped for a few moments alone with. Ney in a little cabin. "Well, Ney," he said, "what do you think of this hut and of our situation? Don't you think we should be lucky if we could be sure of such a retreat for our old age?"

From Villeneuve-l'Archevêque, the march lost its military aspect. Being sure of the safety of the road, he went on ahead of his troops, jumped into a wagon with Caulaincourt and Berthier, and drove swiftly through Moret and Fontainebleau, urging the postilions to full speed. At last, at six in the evening, he reached Fromenteau, but five leagues distant from his capital. He was too late!

What had happened in Paris?

8

Paris at the End of March

In the last days of March Paris was filled with the keenest anxiety. No news was received from the Emperor; it was uncertain whether the enemy was retreating or marching on the capital. The Ministers had no more information than the public, and gloomy forebodings announced the approaching disasters.

One evening the Empress, as was her habit, received a few persons at the Tuileries. Calm and self-controlled, she gave no sign of her distress. She had invited the Duke of Rovigo, but when she had sat down at the card-table she would not let the cards be taken from their case: she no longer cared to play. A few minutes later she took the Duke aside and asked him if he had received any letters from the Emperor. He answered, "No."

"Well," she then said, "I will give you news about him; I heard from him this morning."

And when Savary expressed surprise, saying that no courier had arrived, the Regent added:

That is true; no courier has arrived; and I shall surprise you still more when I tell you that Marshal Blücher has sent me a letter from the Emperor, which, he says, was found with many others on a courier who was captured by the enemy. To tell you the truth, I am very anxious, for I have thought of what may result from this accident. The Emperor, ever since his departure, has written to me in cipher; all these letters have reached me safely; this one, not in cipher, is the only one in which he speaks to me about his plan, and that must be the one to fall into the enemy's hands. There is a fatality about that which makes me very sad.

In this letter Napoleon announced his march to the east, tried to reassure her about the consequences of this movement, and bade her not to be surprised if she should not hear from him for some days. When Marshal Blücher had captured the bearer of this letter, he forwarded the letter to the outposts under a flag of truce, that it might reach the Empress after it had been read by him. It ended with these words: "This step saves me or ruins me."

Marie Louise perfectly understood the extreme gravity of the situation. Without a single adviser capable of reassuring her by his energy, she felt that everything about her was crumbling. She had no confidence in her brothers-in-law; she had seen Napoleon quarrel with them all. She knew how hard he had found it to become reconciled with Joseph, whom she suspected of jealousy of her and of secret intrigue against the Emperor. She knew, also, how annoyed the Emperor had been when, January 1, 1814, Louis had come to Paris without permission and had stayed with his mother.

Then an order had been conveyed to him to move to a distance of forty leagues from the capital, but he refused to obey. "No one," he said, "has any right to prevent my staying at my own house."

It was not till January 10, that, thanks to the Empress's intervention, he was able to get admission to the Emperor. The interview was a cold one; the two brothers did not kiss. "I should prefer that Holland return to the power of the house of Orange rather than to that of my brother." The pacific counsels and wise warnings that he received from Louis during the campaign irritated him extremely.

He never pardoned him for a letter, written March 16, which was simply prophetic, and in which the former King of Holland wrote thus:

If Your Majesty does not sign peace, you may be sure that your government will not last more than three weeks. It needs only a little coolness and common sense to judge the state of affairs.

As for Jerome, Napoleon, before leaving for the field, had refused to receive him at the Tuileries, and, February 4, 1814, the Empress had been forced to write to Joseph:—

My Dear Brother: I have this moment received a letter from the Emperor on the 2nd, in which, in answer to mine, he forbids my receiving on any pretext the King and Queen of Westphalia, in public or *incognito*. Hence I beg of you, my dear brother, to express to them all the regret I feel at not being able to see them tomorrow, and to believe in the sincere friendship with which I am, my dear brother, your affectionate sister.

February 21, Napoleon was somewhat better disposed towards Jerome. That day he wrote from Nogent-sur-Seine to Joseph:—

My Brother: These are my wishes about the King of Westphalia: I authorize him to wear the coat of a grenadier of my guard, the permission I grant to all the French Princes: you will inform King Louis of this. It is absurd for him to wear a Dutch uniform. King Jerome will at once get rid of his Westphalian household. Immediately afterwards, the King and Queen will be presented to the Empress, and I authorize the King to occupy the house of Cardinal Fesch, since it appears to belong to him, and to establish his household there.

The King and Queen will continue to bear the title of King and Queen of Westphalia, but they will have no Westphalian in their suite. When that is done, the King will come to my headquarters, when I intend to send him to Lyons, to take command of that city, of the department and the army, if he will promise to be always at the outposts, and to have no royal retinue, no extravagance, not more than fifteen horses, to bivouac with his soldiers, and not to let a gun be fired without being at the front.

This plan fell through. Like Joseph and Louis, Jerome stayed in Paris until after the Empress had left. Since they inspired no confidence in the Emperor, how could they in her?

Meanwhile, alarm was spreading everywhere, and Paris was in the wildest confusion. With the exception of a few traitors who actually rejoiced in the public misfortunes, the populace was panic-stricken. They were afraid that the city would be sacked, and had but little doubt that it would be burned, like Moscow. When news came that the Emperor Alexander and the King of Prussia had slept at Coulommiers, only fourteen leagues from Paris, and the country people began to drive their herds before them and to throng into the city with such of their belongings as they could load on their carts, the terror was complete.

Idle and discontented patriots wandered through the suburbs and along the boulevards, demanding arms and denouncing the indifference of the government. The disseminators of bad news thronged the cafe's, the theatres,—for the theatres, oddly enough, were not closed,—the streets, and public places, spreading abroad the wildest rumours. There was no one to stop them; there was no police, no government. National resistance, a great popular uprising, was something impossible.

On the battle-field of Arcis-sur-Aube Napoleon had said to General Sébastiani, who asked him why he did not summon the nation to rise:

That's a wild dream based on memories of Spain and the French Revolution. It is useless to call upon a nation in which the Revolution has destroyed the priests and the nobles, and in which I have myself destroyed the Revolution!

Napoleon was right. To defend Paris against two hundred thousand Allies, to protect the city with barricades, to have the tocsin sounded, to determine to conquer or die, required patriotism and religious sentiment. It demanded monks like those of Saragossa, to set the Holy Sacrament before the attacking hordes, and a band of fanatics, like the men who burned Moscow, who chose rather to see the city in flames than in the hands of foreigners.

Paris was moved by a very different feeling,—a yearning for safety. A few heroes swore that they would die before they saw the great capital polluted by the presence of the foreigners; but most of the inhabitants said that Paris could not, should not, and would not be sacrificed merely to prolong the tottering power of the Emperor. The National Guard did not represent the people; it was drawn solely from the middle classes, and even for its scanty members—only about twelve thousand men—there were not more than three thousand muskets. Either through improvidence, or the desire not to alarm the populace, no serious preparations for defence had been made.

There were magnificent fortifications, rich arsenals, abundant troops at Dantzic, Hamburg, Flushing, Palma Nuova, Venice, Alessandria—but in Paris, actually nothing!—no armament, no muskets, no cannon, no fortifications, with the exception of a few wretched palisades in the suburbs. To oppose the two hundred thousand well-trained and fully-equipped invaders there were only about twenty-five thousand men, including the troops of Marshals Marmont and Mortier, who had just reached Charenton, those of General Compans, a few battalions hastily formed from the guards of the public buildings, and finally the twelve thousand National Guardsmen, most of whom were armed only with pikes.

Meanwhile the enemy was advancing; the cannon could heard in the neighbourhood of the capital. What was Marie Louise to do? Should she leave Paris or remain? This question was to be discussed at a council held at the Tuileries in the evening of March 28.

It was one of the most pathetic deliberations recorded in history; and although it resulted in the fall of the Imperial power, the Emperor was unable to blame his councillors, for their determination was in strict accordance with his orders.

The Empress Regent presided over the meeting, at which were present King Joseph; Talleyrand, Prince of Benevento, Vice Grand Elector; Cambacérès, Prince of Parma, Archchancellor; Lebrun, Duke of Piacenza, Archtreasurer; M. de Molé, Chief of Justice; M. de Montalivet, Minister of the Interior; Clarke, Duke of Feltre, Minister of War; M. Bigot de Préameneu, Minister of Worship: M. de Sussy, Minister of Commerce; Champagny, Duke of Cadore, Secretary of State: Gaudin, Duke of Gaëta, Minister of Finance; M. Mollien, Minister of the Public Treasury; M. Daru, Minister of the Administration of War; Savary, Duke of Rovigo, Minister of Police; Duke Decrès, Minister of the Navy; M. de Lacépède, President of the Senate; Régnier, Duke of Massa, President of the Legislative Body; Messrs. Regnault de Saint Jean d'Angély, Boulay (of Meurthe), Merlin (of Douai), Muraire, Cessac, and Fermont, Ministers of State. The meeting began at half-past eight p.m.

The Minister of War, Clarke, Duke of Feltre, was the first to speak.

"Listening to the Minister of War," says the Duke of Rovigo, "it was hard to escape from evil forebodings; his speech was a combination of loyalty, prudence, adulation, and independence, out of which nothing could be made. He seemed to wish to say: 'I have given you full warning; I wash my hands of everything else.'"

Clarke spoke at length of the dangers threatening the capital, on the petty number of its defenders, of the impossibility of the Emperor's arriving in time to save it; and after accompanying this dreary statement with numerous protestations, of untiring devotion, he urged the immediate departure of the Empress and of the King of Rome, who, in his opinion, should be sent at once to the Loire, out of reach of the enemy.

M. Boulay opposed the views of the Minister of War, with great energy. He said that if the capital was left to the influence of the foreigners and the intrigues of the Royalists, all was lost;

that flight would be to set an example for surrender, and would discourage and depress brave men who had sworn to Napoleon to defend his wife and his son; that Paris, without the Empress, would be like a corpse; and that her departure Would be in fact a dissolution of the Regency, and the abdication of the Empire. He added that the Empress, so far from following this pusillanimous advice, should take her son in her arms and show herself to the people, pass through the streets, boulevard, and suburbs, and go to the Hôtel de Ville, to give an example of heroic resolution. The populace would applaud her, and in this solemn moment would repeat what the Hungarians had cried out to her ancestress, Maria Theresa: "*Moriamur pro rege nostro!*"

These eloquent words greatly moved the Council. The Dukes of Rovigo, of Massa, of Cadore, were especially conspicuous for the ardour with which they expressed their approval. King Joseph and Cambacérès said not a word. The Empress, anxious and silent, closely scanned her councillors.

Then Prince Talleyrand spoke. Everyone suspected his fidelity to the Empire, and there was general curiosity to know what this able but dangerous man would advise. He was grave and calm, and spoke with that imposing authority, that dignified self-possession, that slowness which never forsook him, and was astute enough to tell the truth, while preparing for any contingency. He said plainly that the departure of Marie Louise would throw Paris into the hands of the Royalists and would leave the field open for the Coalition to establish a change of dynasty.

The Duke of Rovigo expressed himself in similar terms.

"In support of my opinion," he says in his *Memoirs*, "I spoke of the excellent spirit of that portion of the populace which is the least taken into account though it is untiring in its sacrifices."

Then there were a few moments of silence. The Archchancellor called for a vote, and it was found that there was almost unanimous opposition to the departure of the Empress and of the King of Rome.

However, fuller consideration having been thought advisable, the Duke of Feltre arose, and after a long introduction in which he enumerated some instances from history of fidelity and devotion to sovereigns driven from their capital by war, he went on to say that it was a mistake to regard Paris as the only centre of the Imperial power; that the Emperor's power followed him wherever he might be; that so long as a village was left in which he or his. son was recognized, there all Frenchmen should rally, for that was the real capital.

It was the duty of the Empress and of the King of Rome to go to the uninvaded provinces, there to summon all good men to their banner, and with them to die in defence of the country and the throne. For his part, he could not understand how men who had long professed devotion to the Emperor could advise that his son should be exposed to the chance of falling into the enemy's hands. This was the only bond that united them to Austria, and that they would be helpless if they should follow the perfidious counsel of surrendering Hector's son to the Greeks.

> "The Duke of Feltre," says the Duke of Rovigo, "was much excited; he evidently chose his words to express before the Empress his devotion to the Emperor, and he showed no fear of opposing the whole Council. Moreover, his speech was answered very fully by different councillors, and when the vote was taken again, it was found that no man had changed his opinion that the Empress would do better to stay in Paris."

King Joseph alone had not voted, and up to that moment he kept silence. Then he took the floor and read two letters from Napoleon. One, written after the battle of Rothière, was dated Nogent, February 8, 1814; the other, written after the battles of Craonne and Laon, was dated Rheims, March 16. We have already quoted the first, which ended thus:

> With the Empress and the King of Rome in Vienna, or in the enemy's hands, you and all who tried to defend themselves would be rebels. For my part I had rather my

son should have his throat cut than that I should see him brought up in Vienna as an Austrian prince, and I have a high enough opinion of the Empress to be sure that she shares this opinion so far as a woman and a mother can. I have never seen *Andromaque* played without pitying the fate of Astyanax who survives his family, and without thinking it would have been better for him not to survive his father. You do not know the French people. The results of what would happen in those great events lie beyond calculation.

The reading of this first letter produced a deep impression of discouragement and surprise. The second letter, that of March 16, was even more explicit. Like the other, it was from Napoleon to Joseph; it ran as follows:

In conformity with the oral instructions that I gave you, and with the tendency of all my letters, you must not, in any case, let the Empress and the King of Rome fall into the enemy's hands. I am about to move in such a way that you may possibly be several days without news of me. If the enemy should advance on Paris in such force that resistance would be impossible, despatch towards the Loire the Regent, my son, the high dignitaries, the Ministers, the officers of the Senate, the Presidents of the Council of State, the high officers of the Crown, the Baron de la Bouillerie, and the Treasury. Do not abandon my son, and remember that I had rather know him in the Seine than in the hands of the enemies of France; the fate of Astyanax, a prisoner among the Greeks, has always seemed to me the most melancholy in all history.

When Joseph had finished reading this second letter, the members of the Council gazed at one another in stupefaction. Why had they been summoned if the Emperor's orders were formal? Why ask their opinion if it had been determined already not to follow it? Was this only one of the mockeries of debate of the pretended deliberations of which the Imperial Government had given so many examples? In that case it was easy to understand the Duke of Feltre, who doubtless was already familiar with the two letters, when he so strongly urged the departure of Marie Louise and. her son.

Nevertheless, the members of the Council who were opposed to their leaving still tried to prevent it. M. de Talleyrand repeated what he had already said. Their efforts were vain. King Joseph declared that it was impossible without being guilty of rebellion by disobedience of his brother's precise orders. A third and last vote was taken, and the departure was determined; the Empress, who wished to remain, announced that she and her son could leave at eight the next morning for Rambouillet.

This decision once taken, each minister asked for definite instructions. It was decided that King Joseph should remain in the capital, to superintend the defence, and that he should not leave till it became impossible to save the city from the enemy; that Archchancellor Cambacérès and the President of the Senate should accompany the Empress and the King of Rome; that the other dignitaries, with the Ministers, should remain in Paris until King Joseph should order them to leave, and that this order, to prevent all mistake, should come to them through the Chief Justice, M. de Molé; and finally, that the President of the Senate should write to each member of that body, to avoid obeying any illegal summons. Then at two o'clock in the morning the meeting broke up.

Before leaving the Tuileries, the members of the Council, of whom Marie Louise had just taken leave, stopped in a room next to the one where they had been in session, and some of them came up to Savary and whispered in his ear:

If I were the Minister of Police, like you, Paris would be in insurrection tomorrow, and the Empress would not leave.

The Duke of Rovigo replied:

Which one of you would consent to take the responsibility for what might be the result of such a course, especially when you have just decided that the Emperor's orders must be obeyed? You advise me to take on myself what you have thought you could not do. But do I know the Emperor's plans? Am I even sure that this movement would not thwart them? And if I failed, what good would come from the murders, the pillage, and all the disorders that would follow an appeal to the multitude?

The memory of the Revolution was still fresh, and doubtless Savary had in mind the Jacobins,—the men armed with pikes,—the September massacres, when he wrote:

Is it sure, is it even likely, that the monarch who refused to cover his defeat by burning Leipsic would care to reign at the price of the misfortunes which such a plan would entail upon the capital? How could I reply to his reproaches?

What could I say in answer to the reproaches of a hundred thousand families, one calling for its head, the other for its home, its fortune, all lost through me? There would be too many victims, too many tears: I cannot undertake to throw the whole population of Paris into an abyss. Besides, even if I were strong enough, the spirit of my instructions forbids. So far from wishing me to compromise the populace, the Emperor orders me to leave Paris if the Allies enter. I can easily prevent the Empress's departure; but only a madman would imagine that he could control the results of this violent action.

In my zeal to serve the Emperor I may destroy the few chances left him, and transfer what hopes he has to the profit of a party. It might be thought of, if I had no orders; but everything has been provided for, and I have only to obey the orders I have received. Like everyone else, I regret the decision just taken; but I don't wish to be responsible alone for what you all together have not dared to do.

The members of the Council, seeing that all was over, that the Empire was lost, went down the grand staircase of the Tuileries in the profoundest gloom. At this last moment M. de Talleyrand went up to Savary, and said to him, with mingled irony and melancholy, something like this:

Well, so this is the end of it all, don't you think? Upon my word, we have lost the game with all the cards in our hands. Just see what comes from the stupidity of a few ignorant men who use their influence day in, day out. Really, the Emperor is to be pitied; yet no one will pity him, because his obstinacy in retaining his advisers has no reasonable ground; it is only a weakness which is incomprehensible in a man like him. Just consider what a fall it is!
To be known as the hero of such adventures instead of being the hero of the age! I groan to think of it. What are we to do now? There is no need for everyone to be crushed under the ruins of this edifice. Well, we shall see what will happen. Instead of denouncing me, the Emperor would have done better to judge those who inspired those prejudices; he would have seen that such friends are more dangerous than enemies. What would he say of anyone else who had got into this trouble?

Most of the members of the Council had left the palace; King Joseph, the Archchancellor, and the Minister of War still lingered for a moment. They accompanied the Empress to her private rooms and said a few words to her about the probable melancholy consequences of her leaving Paris. Baron de Méneval, who was present, records that they ventured to say that the Regent alone could determine just what course was to be followed in this serious state of affairs.

"You are my lawful councillors," answered Marie Louise; "I shall not take it upon myself to issue an order opposed to that of the Emperor, and to the determination of the Privy Council, without receiving your opinion in due form and signed."

They refused to take upon themselves such a responsibility. M. de Méneval says in his *Memoirs*:

Now when we can coolly judge the past, can we blame their conduct? If honour and fidelity are not mere words, were they free to sacrifice the man who had trusted to their faith, and to treat with the enemy about him, in his absence? If they had consented to the Emperor's dethronement (for by disobeying his order, they would have committed themselves to that), doubtless the Empress would have secured her son's gratitude, Joseph would have become the lieutenant-general of the kingdom, and the Archchancellor would have retained his dignities, but at what a price?

As she was leaving her councillors, Marie Louise uttered these last words:

Even if I were to fall into the Seine, as the Emperor said, I should not hesitate a moment about leaving. A wish which he has formally expressed is for me an order.

In spite of everything, faint hopes still lingered. Possibly, it was thought, the danger was not so great as it seemed. Perhaps the time for obeying Napoleon's commands had not yet come. Before taking their leave of the Empress, King Joseph and the Minister of War told her that at daybreak the next morning they would both make a military examination outside of Paris, and would send her a last word as to whether she was to go or to stay.

9

The Regent's Flight

The night of March 28 was one of gloom; all sleep in Paris was broken by anxiety and alarm. Belated passers crossing the courtyard of the Carrousel saw in the windows of the Tuileries moving lights, which betrayed the preparation for departure. These preparations were made with eager haste. The bullion in the Treasury and the most precious objects were packed on wagons which were to follow those of the Empress. The morning breeze extinguished the dying lights, when at dawn the early risers noticed with sad surprise the crowd of horses, carriages, and servants. The ladies of Marie Louise wandered distractedly from one room to another. Some old retainers were in tears.

At eight everything was ready for the departure. The travelling-carriages drew up before the Pavilion of Flora, and the rumour quickly spread abroad that the Empress was about to leave. A crowd gathered, and the Place of the Carrousel was soon filled with a multitude of men and women who asked nothing better than to cut the harness, send back the carriages, and to see the Regent share with the Parisians the last chances of fortune. Yet, as the Duke of Rovigo says in his *Memoirs*, so great was still the respect felt for the Empress and for her wishes, that in the whole vast throng all eager to retain her, not one person ventured to express the wish. Yet everyone was thinking:

The departure of Marie Louise is our ruin. Her presence would have guaranteed us against the barbarism of the foreigners. They would never think of sacking, or burning, or bombarding a city in which were the daughter and the son of the Emperor of Austria.

Yet the departure which had been set for eight in the morning did not take place. Marie Louise still hoped she would not have to leave. She was waiting in her room, dressed for the journey, with her son and her ladies, eluding the questions of the little King of Rome, who was much disturbed by the unusual bustle. She expected every moment the report she was to receive from King Joseph, but it did not come. Every sudden noise, a horseman's entrance into the courtyard, the opening of a door, set all hearts throbbing. King Joseph, or one of his messengers, was expected every moment, but no one appeared.

Suddenly the officers of the National Guard, on duty at the Tuileries, and a few other officers—for etiquette could not control the general emotions—burst into the room where was Marie Louise and besought her to remain, promising to defend her and her son to their last breath. Their devotion and earnestness deeply touched the Empress. She felt that they were right in urging her to stay at the Tuileries; she had a foreboding that if she were once to leave the palace she would never enter it again. Her intelligence and common sense told her that this fatal departure was the greatest and most irreparable of faults, and that the fall of the dynasty would be the immediate result. All that she knew, but how could she withstand the Emperor's formal orders, and the insistence of the Minister of War, who sent her word that there was not a moment to lose. Marie Louise thanked the officers of the National Guard, but was obliged to decline their patriotic offers.

Meanwhile, she was waiting most anxiously, fearing both to stay and to go, hoping for another order from the Emperor, a few words from Joseph that the danger was not imminent, and that she might remain a few hours. But nothing came, except a message from the Minister of War saying that she must leave at once; for if there were any delay, she might fall into the hands of the Cossacks.

Eleven struck, and Marie Louise hesitated no longer, but descended the stairs. There her son resisted, and the child of three clung to the doors and banisters, shouting in boyish wrath:

I don't want to leave this house; I don't want to go away; now that papa is away, I'm master here.

The equerry in waiting, M. de Canisy, took him in his arms. He kept struggling and crying:

I don't want to go to Rambouillet; it's an ugly castle; I want to stay here!

And M. de Canisy was obliged to help Madame de Montesquiou to carry him to the carriage in which he was to travel to the first halting-place in his long exile. What is stranger than this child's instinctive repugnance to this journey which was in fact his political death?

The fugitive Empress was accompanied by a numerous suite, comprising the Duchess of Montebello, Madame de Castiglione, Madame de Brignole, and Madame de Montalivet, Count Claude de Beauharnais, Messrs. de Gontaut and d'Haussonville, Prince Aldobrandini, Messrs. d'Héricy and de Lambertye, de Cussy and de Bausset, de Guerehy, Drs. Corvisart, Bourdier, Lacourner, and Royer. The King of Rome was attended by the Countess of Montesquiou, his governess, Madame de Boubers, and Madame de Mesgrigny, M. de Canisy, and Dr. Auvity. The Archchancellor Cambacérès and the President of the Senate followed the Empress. About twelve hundred men, from the reserves of the grenadiers, *chasseurs*, dragoons, and lancers of the Imperial Guard and of the gendarmes formed the escort. They got into their carriages, and the procession started slowly, going out through the gateway near the Pont Royal.

It seemed like the funeral of the Empire! Ten heavy coaches, adorned with the Imperial arms, led the procession, followed by the state coaches, among which was the coronation coach; and then came carts containing rich furniture, records, bullion, silverware, and the crown diamonds. The crowd, which had been dense in the morning, had scattered under the impression that the departure was postponed, and only a few curious idlers lingered near the Tuileries in gloomy silence. When they saw the mounted guards escorting the carriages, they said those men would have been of use in defending the capital, so meagrely garrisoned. The Regent's departure was looked upon as a crime, as a sort of abdication, although it could not properly be blamed, because it was in obedience to orders. But there was no cheering, no expression of sympathy, devotion, or sorrow, as the young and unfortunate Empress was leaving.

Issuing from the gateway by the Pont Royal, the procession followed the quay of the Tuileries. Marie Louise cast a farewell glance at this palace which had proved so fatal; at the Place Louis XV., recalling the scaffold of her aunt, Marie Antoinette; at the Champs Elysées, by which she had entered Paris, four years less four days before, amid pomp and splendour and applause. The Arc de l'Etoile, with its inscriptions and boundless flattery; the speech of the Prefect of the Seine, in which he said:

In order to admire you, we no longer need to trust to report, and already have those words of your immortal husband come true that, loved first for his sake, you would soon be loved for your own

The young girls dressed in white, offering baskets of flowers; the dense crowd in the Champs Elysées; the coronation coach with Marshals of France on horseback by its side; the clanging church bells; the rolling drums; the salutes; applause; the music,—all those things were very remote! One recalls Dante's lines:—

Nessun maggior dolore,
Che ricordarsi del tempo felice
Nella miseria.

The procession advanced along the quay of Chaillot, leaving the capital at Passy to go to Rambouillet. This departure, or rather disastrous flight, made a most melancholy impression on the public, revealing as it did the full extent of the danger threatening Paris; and the gloom was even greater, because hitherto the government bulletins with more cunning than truth, had spoken only of victories over the armies of the Coalition. A few hours before the final crash, the machinery of government was working with apparent regularity.

Two days before there had been a grand review in the courtyard of the Tuileries and in the Place of the Carrousel. For four hours Joseph had watched the parade of the troops of the National Guard, as well as of a numerous force of infantry, cavalry, and artillery, and the Empress and the King of Rome had been cheered when they appeared at a window. In spite of the cloud overhanging the Empire, the theatres remained open.

March 29, the day of the Empress's flight, *Iphigeneia in Aulis* and *Paul and Virgina* were given at the opera; *Manlius* and *The Revenge* at the Français; the *Méfiant* and *J'ai perdu mon procès* at the Odéon; *Le Forgeron de Bassora* and *Richard Cœur-de-Lion* at the Opéra Comique. The smaller theatres were also open. That morning the Parisians had read in the *Moniteur* this military bulletin:

> March 26, His Majesty, the Emperor, defeated General Witzengerode at Saint Dizier, taking two thousand prisoners, many cannon and baggage wagons. The enemy was pursued some distance.

From that time forth the *Moniteur* was silent, saying nothing about the war, about the Empress's flight, or the end of the drama. The number for March 30 was absolutely empty; that of the 31st, purely literary, containing actually nothing of the slightest value, unless we except a *"Fragment of a Journey in Italy, in prose and verse. Pilgrimage to the Festival of the Pardon."*

April 2, the paper opened with a proclamation of the Emperor Alexander. There is nothing more edifying than the number of the *Moniteur* at a change of rule. In an instant the whole tone of the paper is changed. Between one day and the next a century seems to have passed. The reader wonders what has become of the government yesterday so proud, but now vanished like a burst bubble. All rulers ought occasionally to turn over the bound volumes of the *Moniteur Universel;* but no one ever profits by the experience of another.

10

The Battle of Paris

At the same time that Marie Louise was fleeing from the capital, the troops commanded by Marmont and Mortier were hastily crossing the Marne by the bridge of Charenton. In the opposite direction there could be descried from the heights of Montmartre and Belleville, the vanguard of the allied armies, issuing from the woods of Bondy.

> "From the top of the towers of Notre Dame," says Chateaubriand, an eyewitness of this great sorrow, "could be seen the head of the Russian columns, like the first ripple of the sea upon the shore.
>
> I felt what a Roman must have suffered when from the capital he saw the soldiers of Alaric and the old Latin city at his feet, when I looked upon the Russian soldiers and at the old city of the Gauls below me. For centuries Paris had not seen the smoke of an enemy's camp. Paris was the point from which Bonaparte had set forth to wander over the earth; he was returning to it, leaving behind him the enormous flame of his profitless conquests."

March 29, the day of the Empress's flight, at three in the afternoon, the leading columns of the army of Bohemia, under command of Prince Schwarzenberg, occupied Rosny, as well as the lower part of the plateau of Romainville, and halted there under the very erroneous impression that they were confronted by serious obstacles.

The Russian Emperor and the King of Prussia spent the night of March 29 at the castle of Bondy, while the troops of Marmont and Mortier, worn out by incessant fighting and forced marches, took a few hours' rest at Saint Mandé and Charenton before the fierce fight of the next day. Such was the carelessness of the administration that they had nothing to eat, and were obliged to depend on the generosity of the inhabitants. Joseph, who as the Emperor's lieutenant-general was at the head of affairs after the Empress's departure, gave instructions to the two Marshals: Marmont was intrusted with the defence of the capital to and including the heights of Belleville and Ménilmontant; Mortier was to defend the line extending from the foot of these heights to the Seine.

Only a small part of the circumference of Paris is fitted by nature for defence; but this could be utilized, especially since the enemy was advancing in this direction. From the junction of the Marne with the Seine at Charenton, as far as Passy, a chain of hills, at times spreading into plateaus, as at Romainville, at times separate, as at Montmartre, encloses the city. These heights ought to have been covered with redoubts and artillery; but in fact the preparations were most insignificant, consisting only of a few cannon at Montmartre, Saint Chaumont, and Charonne, and of a few palisades before the gates.

No one had thought of raising barricades within the city, of arming the populace with shot-guns, if nothing better was to be had, and of organizing a defence from street to street. As Thiers says,

> Paris should have been defended as General Bourmont, a few days before, had defended Nogent; as General Alix had defended Sens; as the Spaniards had defended their cities; as the Parisians have themselves too often defended Paris against their own governments, with the suburbs barricaded; and the populace behind the barricades and the army of the line in reserve to move on such points as the enemy might have taken.

But it must be confessed that, with a few honourable exceptions, the heroic feeling required for the defence of the capital existed only among the poorer inhabitants. The habit of relying on the strength of the government had weakened all individual initiative. The yearning for security deadened national pride. Suddenly, after being for twenty-two years forgotten, the Bourbons were remembered, and many were asking of what use were the torrents of blood that had been shed since their fall. What some called treachery, others called fidelity. France, in its sore need for harmony in its struggle with the foreigner, was divided against itself. Instead of one flag, under which it might have found safety, it was to have two.

The final resistance was to be in the form of a battle fought under the walls of Paris, which, as Thiers says, was the most foolish plan possible; for, that battle lost, everything was lost,—the battle, Paris, the government, France. To oppose the two hundred thousand excellent troops of the Coalition, they had only twenty-eight or twenty-nine thousand men, among whom were four thousand conscripts, six thousand National Guards, a few hundred *invalides* and young men of the schools.

The Sixth Corps, under Marmont, which was to bear the brunt of the attack, consisted of but four thousand seven hundred and thirty-one men, of whom fourteen hundred and twenty-one were mounted. They were mere fragments, shadows of regiments ready to die in defence of their flag. This was the sixty-seventh engagement of the Sixth Corps, since January 1, that is to say, in ninety days; and its commander, Marmont, Duke of Ragusa, had worn his arm in a sling throughout the whole campaign, in consequence of a wound he had received in Spain; two fingers of his other hand were wounded, so that he had to hold his sword with but three fingers.

March 30, an hour before day, General Marmont left Charenton to form in line of battle. At six o'clock a Russian cannon announced the last battle of the Empire. At that moment the Parisians were reading this proclamation of King Joseph, which had been posted everywhere:

105

King Joseph, lieutenant-general of the Emperor, commander-in-chief of the National Guard, to the citizens of Paris: A column of the enemy is moving on Meaux, advancing by the road to Germany, but the Emperor is following it closely at the head of a victorious army. The Council of the Regency has provided for the safety of the Empress and of the King of Rome. Let us arm in defence of our city, of its monuments, of its treasures, of our wives, of our children, of all that we hold dear. This vast city should become for a brief space a camp, and the enemy must suffer humiliation beneath the walls which he hopes to overthrow in triumph! The Emperor is marching to our aid; help him by a brief and vigorous resistance, and let us maintain the honour of France.

At six in the morning Joseph and his brother Jerome had ridden to Montmartre to watch the movements of the enemy.

Meanwhile, Marmont's troops had taken position on the heights of Belleville and Ménilmontant. The enemy in front of Romainville were so hotly attacked that they thought that Napoleon must have arrived, and they cautiously remained on the defensive. The French line was formed with the left at the mill of Romainville, holding all the little wood, and with the right at the passes on the top of Bagnolet and at the mill of Malassise.

The battle raged hotly for some hours, and until eleven neither side gained any substantial advantage; at that hour, however, the Allies attacked in great numbers, and the French line was forced. Marmont and his troops were obliged to withdraw a little more than half a mile, to the village of Belleville, with the right at Ménilmontant, and the left by the meadows of Saint Gervais. The roads to Paris were blocked with a number of wounded Frenchmen. From all sides arose a call for aid, but Marmont still held firm.

It was nearly noon. Joseph, when he found that nearly all the armies of the Coalition were engaged, and that Napoleon was not coming, thought the case hopeless. Montmartre, where he was with his escort, was soon to be attacked. With fifty pieces of artillery it could have been defended; but as it was, there were but seven cannon and a handful of the National Guard.

Fearing to be taken as a hostage and possibly compelled to bring about the Emperor's dethronement, Joseph, in spite of the proclamation he had issued that morning, thought of but one thing,—of leaving the capital and rejoining Marie Louise with a shadow of a government. Hence he wrote to Count Molé, the Chief Justice:

> Count, I think you should notify the Ministers that it is proper for them to follow in the steps of the Empress. Inform the Senators and the Councillors of State, etc.

And he wrote to the Duke of Piacenza:

> Sir: I think it is proper for the high dignitaries to withdraw from Paris, in the steps of the Empress, on the road to Chartres. Be good enough to inform the dignitaries.

At quarter-past twelve Joseph sent by his aide, General Stroltz, to Marshal Marmont and then to Marshal Mortier, permission to treat with the enemy, in these words:

> If the Marshal, the Duke of Ragusa, and the Duke of Treviso are no longer able to hold their positions, they are authorized to treat with Prince Schwarzenberg and the Emperor of Russia, who are before them. They will retreat on the Loire.

When Marmont received this paper, he bade one of his aides go to tell Joseph that if the rest of the line was in no worse state than where he was, he did not think the time had come for capitulation, and that he still hoped to hold out till night, when perhaps there might be a change. Although his valiant corps was nearly wiped out by six hours' fighting, Marmont would not give up.

> "He was," says General de Ségur, "one of the oldest companions of the great captain; this was the last battle of the remnants of the Grand Army, the last moment of the inde-

pendence of the capital and of the great nation; he knew that all these grandeurs could not fall like so many others, that there was need of other sacrifices, of bloodier funeral rites, and he dedicated himself to them. He did more; he made all who were with him unite in this heroic devotion; for not a man left him. Yet far on the right another army, under the Prince of Würtemberg, was turning his position, while Blücher was pressing his left. Already, in spite of the desperate defence made by a few hundred conscripts and the pupils of the Veterinary School of Alfort, Saint Maur and Charenton had been turned and taken; Bercy was captured; the Würtembergers had already got by Vincennes, and before the Barrière du Trône, the reserve artillery and the pupils of the Polytechnic School had been turned back. Twenty-one of these pupils had just paid with their blood for the fame that their devotion added to the renown of this school."

Mortier was defending himself boldly at Villette, and Marmont at Belleville. Six times had the latter's troops lost and six times retaken important points in their front line, among others, the little towns flanking the walls of the Park of Bruyères. The brave marshal fought like a lion. His clothes were torn by bullets, and his horse had been shot under him. With but a handful of brave men, he was fighting desperately in the main street of Belleville. Never had soldiers fought more obstinately, but a prolongation of the struggle was impossible.

The enemy learned from the prisoners by how small a force they were opposed, and at length perceived that they could advance without danger; consequently, immense bodies began to move forward. From the heights of Belleville could be seen huge columns of fresh troops advancing from all sides—from the Barrière du Trône to Villette, while other troops were crossing the canal of the Ourcq and moving on Montmartre. It was half-past three o'clock.

Marmont saw that if Paris was to be saved from the horrors of assault, the time for negotiating had come. A little before four he sent a first flag of truce, preceded by a trumpeter, to propose a suspension of hostilities. Colonel de La Bédoyère, who had been entrusted with this perilous mission, soon returned; he had not been able to advance; his horse and that of the trumpeter had been killed. The combat was too hot at that point for a flag of truce to have any success. Then Marmont sent an *aide-de-camp* to General Compans, who had a new place for entering into communication with the enemy, being in the front line, at the foot of the hills of la Villette, at the entrance of the highroad, and he ordered him to try to open negotiations.

At the same moment a horseman appeared among the troops of the Duke of Treviso, who was stoutly defending la Villette. It was an *aide-de-camp* of the Emperor, General Dejean, who had come to say that Napoleon was moving on Paris at full speed, and that it was only necessary to hold out two days more when he would appear at the head of a considerable force; that hence every effort should be made to prolong the defence, and if this could not be done by arms, the enemy was to be delayed by discussions, and was to be told that the Emperor had written to his father-in-law to ask for a reopening of negotiations.

When Mortier's troops saw General Dejean, they thought that Napoleon had arrived. A loud cry of "Long live the Emperor!" arose, and the soldiers fought with fresh fury. Meanwhile, the bearer of the first flag of truce sent by General Compans, in accordance with Marmont's orders, had been killed, and the second severely wounded. The third, M. de Quélen, had been able to reach Prince Schwarzenberg, who at once consented to an immediate conference about a suspension of hostilities. This conference, in which took part Marmont and Mortier, and the representatives of the Allies, Messrs. de Nesselrode, Orloff, and Paar, was held in the second house on the left of the gate of la Villette. It was a restaurant called *au Petit Jardinet*.

During the conference the battle raged as hotly as ever. Life in Paris was not modified by these dreadful events. From the moment the battle began, the boulevards had been crowded by men standing and sitting, who discussed what was going on. In the wealthy quarters patriotism was much less prominent than it was in the suburbs, and there were abundant indications of the indifference which was to prevail the next day. Montmartre, which was defended only by General Belliard's cavalry and two hundred and forty firemen, had just been carried by one of Blücher's army corps, commanded by a Frenchman, General Langeron; and when they had secured this important position, the Allies at once turned their guns on the capital. At about half-past four shells and cannon-balls began to fall in what is now the Quarter of the Chaussée d'Antin, and a general bombardment seemed imminent.

Chateaubriand says of their last hour:

> The crowd hurried to the Jardin des Plantes, which the fortified abbey of Saint Victor might have protected; the little home of the swans and the banana-trees, to which our power had promised eternal peace, was disturbed. From the top of the labyrinth, above the great cedar, above the storehouses which Bonaparte had not had time to finish, beyond the site of the Bastille and of the dungeon of Vincennes (places full of historical memories), the multitude watched the combat of Belleville. Montmartre was carried, and bullets reached the *boulevard du* Temple.
>
> A few companies of the National Guard sallied forth and lost three hundred men in the 'fields about the tombs of the martyrs. Never did the military spirit of France shine in a brighter light in defeat; the last heroes were five hundred young men of the Polytechnic School, who were directing the artillery in the Vincennes redoubts. Though surrounded by the enemy, they refused to yield: they had to be dragged away from their guns. The Russian Grenadiers seized them blackened with powder and covered with wounds; while they struggled in their arms there rose cries of victory and admiration for the young French heroes, who were handed, covered with blood, to their mothers.

Alas! this glorious resistance was at an end. Everything has its limits, even heroism. Twenty-two years of unprecedented triumph ended in this chivalrous and mournful way. The death-roll attests the obstinate rally of the defenders of Paris; of twenty-four thousand killed and wounded, there were six thousand French soldiers, nine hundred National Guards, and more than seventeen thousand of the foreigners.

At five in the evening the conference about the suspension of hostilities was drawing to a close. To an insulting request to lay down their arms, the two marshals answered by a gesture of indignant scorn; when it was proposed that they leave Paris and take the road to Brittany, they answered that they would go where they pleased. The sole condition they accepted was to evacuate Paris in the night and to surrender the gates in the morning. It was agreed that the officers would meet in the evening to settle the details of the evacuation, and shortly after five the suspension of hostilities was determined.

Still all was not over. While the discussion was going on, the Allies, who were masters of Montmartre, advanced as far as the Clichy gate. There they found a brave veteran, a man of sixty, Marshal Moncey, Duke of Conegliano, Major-General of the National Guard of Paris. About him were grouped citizen-soldiers as brave and devoted as the Spartans of Leonidas at Thermopylæ. Old men and young, *invalides,* students, were serving the artillery outside of the gate. The armistice had just been concluded, but the Allies, doubtless ignorant of the fact, attacked the little phalanx. The National Guard defended themselves like lions. The *rue de* Clichy was covered with barricades. Then the suspension of hostilities was announced; but the Russians made what seemed an offensive movement, and the National Guard reopened their fire, which Langeron and Moncey hastened to stop.

Those who admire this noble end of so many glories will recall the monument raised in commemoration of this proud memory. On a huge stone pedestal stands the bronze statue of Marshal Moncey, bareheaded, sword in hand. Above him stands the city of Paris, represented by a beautiful woman, whose head is adorned by a mural crown; she holds in her hand a standard decorated with an eagle; at her feet a dead National Guardsman lies stretched over a cannon with broken wheels. On one side of the pedestal is this inscription:

In the reign of Napoleon III., in, memory of the defence of Paris by Marshal Moncey, Major-General of the National Guard, March 30, 1814, at the Clichy gate, this monument has been erected by the city of Paris in 1869.

On the other side of the pedestal is reproduced in stone the famous picture of Horace Vernet,—that impressive, heroic picture, of which the Restoration was as much afraid as of Béranger's songs.

11

Napoleon at the Fountains of Juvisy

March 30, 1814, at about ten in the evening, post-horses galloped into the village of Fromenteau, five leagues from the capital, near the Fountains of Juvisy, drawing a modest carriage. In
this carriage sat a man who, with feverish anxiety, was counting
the minutes, the seconds, and continually urging on the *postilion*.
This man was Napoleon, who was accompanied by Caulaincourt and Berthier. He had pushed on ahead of his troops, hoping to reach Paris in season.

When he stopped to change horses at Fromenteau he knew
nothing of what had taken place that day and the day before,—
nothing of the flight of his wife and son, nothing of the battle of
Paris and of the capitulation. All was lost, and he was still hoping
that all could be saved. He was expecting news in the most painful anxiety, when suddenly, in the dim light, he descried uni-
forms. To his great surprise he saw before him General Belliard.
"What! you, Belliard?" he exclaimed. "What does this mean?
You here with your cavalry? Where is the enemy?"

"At the gates of Paris, Sire."

"And the army?"

"It is following me."

"And who are guarding the capital?"

"The National Guard, Sire."

"And my son, my wife, my government—where are they?"

"On the Loire."

"The Loire! How could they make such a decision?"

"But, Sire, it was said to be done by your orders."

"And Joseph, Clarke, Marmont, Mortier,—what has become of them? What have they done?"

Then General Belliard described everything that had happened that day and the day before,—the departure of Marie Louise and the King of Rome, that of Joseph and the Ministers, the bloody battle of Paris, the terrible struggle of la Villette and Belleville, the suspension of hostilities determined at five o'clock the previous evening, the capitulation, the clause of which at that very moment Marmont was about drawing up.

Then Napoleon understood why General Belliard happened to be at the Fountains of Juvisy. Belliard was in command of the cavalry of Mortier's army corps, and had been fighting bravely all day. After the signing of the armistice Marmont and Mortier ordered that the troops who were compelled to evacuate the city should move towards Fontainebleau. Ever since the two marshals had joined forces Marmont had continually been in front in advancing on the enemy and at the rear in retreating, up to the suppression of hostilities.

Mortier's corps had set out first on the road to Fontainebleau, while Marmont's bivouacked that night in the Champs Elysées, to start at seven the next morning. At last Napoleon grasped the full extent of the catastrophe. General Belliard set before him the excellent conduct of the troops, the really heroic obstinacy with which they had defended the hills commanding Paris. He said that even Montmartre had been defended, although he had only his cavalry, a few firemen, and seven cannon, and that the enemy had advanced a column along the road of the Révolte to turn Montmartre, thereby exposing itself to being driven into the Seine.

"O Sire!" he exclaimed, "if we had only had a reserve of ten thousand men, we should have driven the Allies into the Seine, have saved Paris, and had a noble revenge."

"Doubtless, if I had been there, but I couldn't be everywhere! My two hundred cannon at Vincennes, what was done with them? and my brave Parisians, why were they not made use of?"

"We don't know, Sire. We were alone, and we did our best. The enemy lost at least twelve thousand men."

"It's what I might have expected. Joseph lost me Spain, and is losing me France! But there is no need of complaining; we must make good the harm; there is still time. Caulaincourt, my carriage!"

The carriage did not come, and Napoleon was greatly agitated, pacing up and down with long strides, followed by General Belliard. "Well," he said, "you hear what I say. I mean to go to Paris."

"But, Sire, you will not find a French soldier there."

"That makes no difference; I shall find the National Guard there. Tomorrow, or next day, my army will join me, and I shall set things straight." And in even greater agitation the Emperor continued to pace up and down. Belliard tried to convince him that this was an idle dream; that an insurmountable difficulty stood in his way,—the absence of his army.

The troops who had defended Paris were bound by the agreement made the previous evening not to leave a single soldier within its gates, so Napoleon would be alone. "What difference does that make?" he shouted angrily. "I mean to go to Paris, and to Paris I go. My carriage! Bring my carriage!"

Belliard respectfully suggested that since he had left Paris under the terms of the convention, he could not return thither without infringing them. Besides, the Emperor would find the enemy at the gates of the capital, and they would prevent his entering. The Emperor's arrival would be the signal of a bombardment. "Let us be off," repeated the furious monarch; "I mean to go to Paris. When I am away, everything is muddled."

Napoleon continued to call for his carriage, and as he paced to and fro broke out in lamentations and the severest recriminations. Why had not a general levy been made in Paris? Why had they not built fortifications, palisades, earthworks, furnished them with artillery, and entrusted them to the National Guard, which would have defended them bravely? Meanwhile the troops of the line might have fought before the city, on the heights, and in the plain. What! only a few wretched palisades at the gates? Only seven guns on Montmartre? What had become of the artillery? There ought to be provisions for a month in Paris, and more than two hundred heavy guns for its defence. Belliard told the Emperor that he had seen only field-pieces, and these were so inefficient that at two o'clock they could only be fired seldom lest they should burst. Then Napoleon raised his eyes to heaven and denounced his brother.

Might he not have blamed himself as well? Might it not have been said to him, "Why didn't you yourself have those defences made, under your own eyes, when the invasion began? Why did you refuse to admit that the capital might someday be attacked? Why did you leave so few of the National Guard? Why didn't you have fifty thousand muskets to distribute among the Parisians? Why did you add to the danger instead of diminishing it? You fancied Paris impregnable, and now it is taken."

Troops were seen advancing; not cavalry, but the infantry of Mortier's corps. The Emperor, still pacing the road, recognized General Curial, and plied him with questions. This officer corroborated all that Belliard had said. Marshal Mortier, as well as Marmont, was still in Paris, and neither the infantry nor the cavalry could return thither. Napoleon found himself without a single soldier; this cavalry and this infantry were of no use to him. Convinced by the evidence, he stopped at the two fountains near Juvisy, sat down, and for a few moments sadly and silently held his head in his hands.

"Where is the nearest shelter?" he then asked. He was told it was at the post-station of Fromenteau, where his carriage had stopped. He returned to the house and went in; then, by the dim light of a wretched lamp, he opened his map and began to study it.

He said, "If I had my army here, all could be made good. Alexander will show himself to the Parisians. He is not bad; he doesn't want to burn Paris. He will hold a review tomorrow, and will have half of his soldiers on the right bank of the Seine, and the other half on the left; there will be some in Paris, some outside; and in this position, if I only had my army, I could crush them all."

Someone said that the army would not arrive for four days.

"Four days!" he went on; "oh! in two days, and in Paris, how much disloyalty! The Empress herself! Yes, I wanted her to go, for Heaven knows what her inexperience might not have led her to do!"

Then he began to pore over the map again, and in a few moments again raised his head, his face afire with sudden inspiration, and cried out: "I've got them! I've got them! God has placed them in my hands. But I must have four days. Caulaincourt, you can gain me these four days by negotiating. You will go to the Emperor Alexander."

"Sire," replied Caulaincourt, "would it not be well to negotiate seriously, to yield to circumstances, if not to men, and to accept the Châtillon proposals, at least the main ones?"

"No, no! "answered the Emperor. "No further humiliations! no shameful peace! This concerns the greatness of France, its honour. This can only be finally settled by the sword. I only want four days. You alone can get them from Alexander in face of all the intrigues that will beset me. So go at once. As for me, I am going to Fontainebleau to wait for you and the army, and to prepare to avenge this momentary humiliation of France."

Caulaincourt started for Paris, carrying the following paper, signed by Napoleon:

We command the Duke of Vicenza, our Master of the Horse and Minister of Foreign Affairs, to visit the allied sovereigns and the commander-in-chief of their armies, to recommend to them our faithful subjects of the capital. By these presents we invest him with all power to negotiate and conclude peace, promising to ratify whatever he may do for the good of our service.

In case of need, we also invest him with military powers, to be the governor and commissioner of this good city together with the commander-in-chief of the Allies. Accordingly we order every official to recognize the Duke of

Vicenza in the said position, and to aid him in all that he shall do for the benefit of our service and of our people.

At the same time Napoleon despatched a messenger to the Emperors. Then, utterly exhausted,—for he had travelled for sixty leagues on horseback and by post, without stopping,—he fell asleep in a wretched chair. At about four in the morning he was awakened by a bearer of despatches from Paris, who brought him word that Marmont had finally concluded the capitulation two hours before.

This paper was signed by four colonels: Colonel Orloff, an *aide-de-camp* of the Emperor of Russia; Colonel Paar, Prince Schwarzenberg's aide; Colonel Fabvier, of the staff of the Duke of Ragusa; and Colonel Denys, this marshal's first *aide-de-camp*. It was agreed that the French troops should evacuate Paris at seven in the morning, that hostilities should not be renewed till two hours later, that is to say, March 31, at 9 a.m.; that the National Guard should be maintained, disarmed, or disbanded, as the Allies might determine; that the wounded men or stragglers who remained in Paris after 7 a.m. should be prisoners of war; finally, the city was entrusted to the generosity of the Powers.

Illusions were no longer possible. The Emperor perceived that it was useless for him to think of leaving for Paris. The Allies, coming down from the heights of Vincennes, had forced the bridge of Charenton and occupied the plain of Villeneuve Saint George; their bivouac fires lit tip the hills on the right bank, while the other side, on which was Napoleon, was dark. Hence he decided to start at four, in his carriage, not for Paris, but for Fontainebleau.

12

The Regency in Flight

Meanwhile, what had become of Marie Louise? Possessing a mere shadow of government, she bore more likeness to a fugitive than to a sovereign. She was uncertain where she should stop, at Blois, at Orléans, or at Tours. Everything was dark and vague before her. As we said, she left Paris, March 29, at eleven in the morning, and reached the castle of Rambouillet the same day; there she passed the night. An eye-witness, the Baron de Bausset, who accompanied the Empress as her Prefect of the Palace, says in his *Memoirs*:

Certainly nothing was less like a court journey than this tumultuous retreat of people and luggage. However, when they were once assembled in the castle of Rambouillet, every one tried to hide the depression which was inspired by the critical state of affairs which threatened the ruin of the government and of the court. This flight was certainly remarkable in many ways.

Everyone was at his post, in full dress, and there was no modification of the usual formality. The minutest rules of etiquette were observed with scrupulous care, as if this could delay their overthrow. The last thing talked about was the events of the day and what might happen on the morrow. Nothing betrayed the secret thoughts and feelings of the company.

It seems as if courtiers, in adversity as well as in prosperity, regarded it as a professional duty to hide the truth from princes.

"Yet," M. de Bausset goes on, "there was one good trait in this side of the manners of the court, and that was the care taken to keep from the Empress all knowledge of the desertions of former friends, of the bad results of her flight, and of the successive blows received by the Imperial power. The ranks closed, and thus formed about the Empress and her son, a band of persons full of the most honourable and most disinterested devotion."

However disinterested the devotion may appear, it is not to be forgotten that, March 29, 1814, the cause of Marie Louise and of the King of Rome did not yet seem hopeless. Nothing was more uncertain than the return of the Bourbons, and many who thought it impossible that Napoleon should longer reign, regarded the accession of his son, with Marie Louise as Regent, as a not merely possible, but very probable contingency. Possibly this last illusion inspired some of the obsequious zeal of these courtiers of the fleeing Empress.

March 30, she left Rambouillet and spent the night at Chartres, without any news of the battle of Paris or of the Emperor. King Joseph, who had left the capital at four in the afternoon, shortly before the battle ended, reached Chartres that night, and received the next day a letter which Napoleon had written just before leaving Fromenteau. The same day at five in the afternoon Joseph wrote to his brother:—

Sire: I sent you this morning a letter by a disguised messenger. This evening I receive Your Majesty's letter of this morning. I forward to the Empress the one addressed to her. I shall leave tonight to join her. She ought to have gone first to Tours. In accordance with Your Majesty's commands, she will go, with the government, to Blois. That is also the opinion of the Ministers who are here, and leave this evening.

The Empress and the King of Rome are very well; I saw them this morning. This evening they will be at Châteaudun. The Ministers of War, of the Administration of the War, of Finance, of the Treasury, of the Interior, of the Navy, are here. Your Majesty must have heard from the marshals everything that has happened, and by what I said to M. Dejean, Your Majesty's *aide-de-camp*. The enemy's force was very great. The Dukes of Treviso and of Ragusa could not resist it.

March 31, Marie Louise slept at Châteaudun, and reached Vendôme April 1. The next morning she left this place for Blois. From Vendôme, April 2, at 11 a.m., Joseph wrote to Napoleon:—

Sire: The Empress has just left for Blois, where she means to stop tomorrow to let her escort and the horses rest. She exhibits a calmness and a courage exceptional in her sex and her age. I am waiting for horses and my family before leaving. The Ministers of the Interior and of War are writing to Your Majesty. The state of the departments is such that I do not doubt that Your Majesty will do anything to make peace. The Ministers and courtiers whom I see exhibit firmness and devotion.

I have received only two letters in cipher. Since neither M. Campi nor M. d'Hauterive has arrived, I have been unable to read them. The Archchancellor left shortly before the Empress. After your letter of the 21st, I did not receive any till that of the 31st. The Archchancellor has received a letter from M. de Bassano, in accordance with which he means to assemble the Ministers. He has read it to the Empress as well as to me.

It will be hard for all the Ministers to meet at Blois tomorrow evening. So far only those of War and of Interior have arrived; none have any decided opinions; their information is too meagre, and they seem to desire that Your Majesty should in his wisdom appoint the most suitable resting-place, which can only be determined by the military conditions. I enclose a package from the Minister of the Interior, with despatches from the Viceroy.

The same day, April 2, Joseph wrote likewise from Vendôme, to Marshal Berthier, who was at Fontainebleau with Napoleon:

I have your letter of March 31, from Fontainebleau. We shall be at Blois this evening. The Ministers of the Interior and of War are replying to Your Highness. The lack of arms still prevails. The other Ministers will not reach Blois before tomorrow. The Empress has left to get there this evening. I hope at Blois to hear from Your Highness and to learn the Emperor's positive decision about the destination of the court and the government. I beg Your Highness to have confidence in my old and lasting friendship. In one word: everything here indicates the need of peace. If it is possible to treat, it must be done at any price. The Royalists are beginning to show themselves; peace of any sort will destroy a party that a continuation of the war will make dangerous.

Marie Louise had a wretched journey from Vendôme to Blois. It rained in torrents; the roads were bad, and the carriages were out of repair. In the morning of Saturday, April 2, the first detachments of cavalry began to arrive at Blois, soon followed by the baggage-wagons and by the fifteen wagons with the contents of the Treasury. At about three in the afternoon the Prefect of the Department set forth to meet the Empress and the King of Rome. The National Guard and the governors were under arms on each side of the road. At five o'clock, Marie Louise and her son entered the city amid an immense multitude, which remained perfectly silent.

The leading citizens and the officials, especially those who lived nearest the prefecture, had been invited to prepare lodging for Madame Bonaparte, Napoleon's mother, for Kings Joseph, Louis, and Jerome; for the Archchancellor, the Ministers, the principal officials, and finally, for eighteen hundred soldiers. The city of Blois rises in the form of an amphitheatre, on the left bank of the Loire. The prefecture crowns one of the ends of this amphitheatre, and is reached only by very steep streets, or by flights of more than a hundred steps. The Ministers, who lived in the lower part of the city, had to climb these steps. Cambacérès, who lived half-way up, took a sedan-chair to go to the prefecture.

Then Marie Louise saw herself surrounded by a whole government, or rather the image of a government, composed of her three brothers-in-law, the wives of Joseph and of Jerome, and of the Ministers. Archchancellor Cambacérès preserved all the customary rigidity of etiquette. Arrayed in his uniform, and wearing his orders, he gravely gave formal audiences.

"The Empress," says the Baron de Bausset, "presided over the councils of the Regency with an exactitude all the more meritorious because they led to nothing: there was no hope of safety there. The palace was like a sort of headquarters; the Ministers, booted and spurred, went thither in undress uniform, without a portfolio, as if they only awaited a word to mount their horses to put the orders they should receive into execution. Nevertheless, since diplomatic forms never relax their rigidity, even in the most distressing circumstances, nothing came from the discussions that took place, probably, too, because in such a state of affairs there was nothing to say."

April 2, Napoleon wrote from Fontainebleau to Joseph:

I have sent you word by the Grand Marshal not to fill up Blois. Let the King of Würtemberg go into Brittany or towards Bourges. I think it would be well for my mother to join her daughter at Nice, and for Queen Julia and her children to go to Marseilles. The Princess of Neufchâtel and the wives of the Marshals ought to go to their estates. It is natural that King Louis, who always likes to live in hot countries, should go to Montpelier.

It is important to have as few people as possible on the Loire, and that everyone should get settled without making any disturbance. Every large colony always upsets the inhabitants more or less. The road to Provence is open, but may be closed any day. In the memorandum of the Ministers you say nothing of the Minister of Police. Has he come? I don't know whether the Minister of War has his cipher. I have none with you, and in the lack of it cannot write on matters of importance. Urge on all the most rigid economy.

Joseph, April 3, thus replied: —

Sire: I have yours of the 2nd. Mamma and Louis are ready to follow your wishes. She will need money; her pension is six months, in arrears. Jerome, too, has no money. My wife has no one at Marseilles. Expenses are much swollen by the fine carriages of the court. I have received no letter from the Grand Marshal on that subject or on any other. The Minister of Police has arrived here on his way back from Tours. Today's council was unanimous in its opinion and wishes.

We await Your Majesty's decision about the place of residence. May the fears spread abroad by the news of the Duke of Vicenza prove groundless! The Minister of War has no cipher with Your Majesty, neither have I. The Minister of the Treasury and of Finance do not know how to use theirs. M. de la Bouillerie would like to have orders about the safety of his charge. One of the wagons containing two millions, which had been left in Paris when the Empress started, has reached Orléans. Might not Jerome be sent to command the army of Lyons?

As for King Louis, he kept himself in obscurity, appearing interested in nothing but the performance of the religious duties of Holy Week, which was just beginning. Palm Sunday, April 3, Marie Louise heard mass, which was said by Abbé Gallois, priest of the parish of Saint Louis; for there was no almoner, chaplain, or clerk of the Imperial chapel in her suite. Poor woman! she needed all her prayers to support the misfortunes now encompassing her.

13

Napoleon at Fontainebleau

One who visits Fontainebleau for the first time is sure to be filled with admiration and surprise. Especially is this true if the weather is fine and the palace is lit up by the sun. Then one is tempted to say: Happy are those who live in this beautiful spot! But afterwards, as one grows familiar with the place, this first impression gives way to one of sadness; one recalls melancholy memories of the famous personages who have dwelt here, and is filled with pity for what they have suffered in these sumptuous halls, and this loveliest of French palaces inspires a profound melancholy.

This was certainly our impression on the occasion of our last visit, which took place on the 14th of July, the anniversary of the taking of the Bastille. That evening, the lanterns lit the Horseshoe Staircase, down which Napoleon came to press the eagle of the standard to his heart, and to take his memorable farewell of the grenadiers of his guard. This Courtyard of the White Horse is certainly not the most beautiful of the castle. It has far less architectural beauty than the Courtyard of the Fountain or the Oval Courtyard. Its façade, composed of five three-storied pavilions with pointed roofs, lacks majesty.

The great staircase, called from its shape the Horseshoe Staircase, is too heavy for the meagre pavilion on which it rests. The two wings, one of four stories, the other of but one, are very dissimilar, and that on the right, built by the architects of Louis XV., with no artistic feeling, is more like a barrack than a palace.

Yet why is this courtyard always so impressive? Because one always recalls Horace Vernet's famous picture, and thinks of Napoleon coming down this staircase, pressing General Petit to his breast, kissing the eagle of the banner, and uttering that speech of which the echo will resound forever.

As you enter the gateway you come into the vast Courtyard of the White Horse, so called from a plaster horse, moulded by Catharine de Medici after the statue of Marcus Aurelius in Rome, which stood in the middle of the courtyard till 1626. To the right is the new wing built by Louis XV.; on the left is the wing of the ministers. At the end of this large court, which measures five hundred feet by a little over two hundred, the façade comes into view with its five pavilions; before the middle one is the Horseshoe Staircase, built in the reign of Louis XIII. Passing beneath this staircase you enter a vestibule on the ground floor, opening, on the left, into the chapel of the Holy Trinity built by Francis I. on the site of the oratory of Saint Louis. This is the best place for beginning the inspection of the palace.

On leaving the chapel you are once more in the vestibule, and a flight of stairs takes you to the apartments of Napoleon I., all the rooms of which open on the Garden of Diana. First is the ante-chamber of the ushers, with three windows; then the room of the Emperor's secretaries, with two; then two small rooms, each with one window; a drawing-room with two windows, which is decorated with red hangings: this is called the drawing-room of the abdication. In the middle of the room stands a little mahogany table; if you tip it a little, you will see that there has been set in it a copper plate bearing this inscription, which is said to have been composed by Louis XVIII.:

> April 5, 1814, Napoleon Bonaparte signed his abdication on this table, in the King's workroom, the second from the bedchamber at Fontainebleau.

Louis XVIII. took a sort of satisfaction in affirming that the man whom he had always regarded as a usurper had signed his abdication in the royal workroom. In this same room Louis

Philippe had placed on a bracket a facsimile of the abdication. This was suppressed during the Second Empire, but it now stands in a glass case at the end of the Gallery of Diana. Next to this room is the Emperor's study, connected by a narrow staircase with his private library, on the ground-floor next to his bedroom.

This room has two windows; the fireplace is in the style of the time of Louis XVI.; the furniture is covered with Lyons velvet, with everywhere a gold N.; the candelabra represent winged Victories; on the walls Loves are painted; the doors are carved and covered with gilt; the clock is of marble with cameos inserted, a gift of Pius VII.: the whole appearance of the room is very impressive. It recalls, too, the sufferings of the great man who occupied it, his sleepless nights in which he endured anguish only equalled by his previous successes, his agony when he had tried to kill himself in despair.

The room looks out on the Garden of Diana, called also the Garden of the Orange House, which lies between the palace and a high wall that intercepts the view of the distance. It is called the Garden of Diana after a statue of that goddess which stands there above a bronze fountain. This fountain was built in the First Empire, but its marble basin had been already hollowed by Henri IV. The garden is somewhat gloomy; on the right stands the chapel of the Holy Trinity, on the left is the old Gallery of the Stags, a melancholy construction, which seems haunted by the ghost of the unhappy Marquis Monalderchini, who was so tragically put to death here by Queen Christine of Sweden.

On the other side, Napoleon's rooms open into the gallery of Francis I. This magnificent gallery, which is as long as the Courtyard of the Fountain is broad, is to the Palace of Fontainebleau what the Gallery of the Mirrors is to that of Versailles. There it was that, in the first twenty days of April, 1814, his faithful officers and his last courtiers used to gather.

This is the gallery which Napoleon passed through before going down the Horseshoe Staircase to bid farewell to his guard. It opens on a terrace with eight windows, where he often walked, seeing, on his right, the rooms of the Pope, so long his prisoner, where he uttered the words we shall soon cite. From there, too, he could see the sheet of water at the end of the Courtyard of the Fountain, bounded on one side by the walk of Madame de Maintenon, on the other by the English garden.

Starting again from the Emperor's bedroom, we pass into the Council Hall with its charming pictures by Boucher and Van Loo. Next is the Throne Room, the former royal bedchamber, with its magnificent chandelier of rock crystal, the Imperial throne of red velvet, ascended by three steps, above which hangs a canopy supported by gold columns.

Beyond is the *boudoir* of Marie Antoinette, with a picture of Aurora adorning the ceiling, and the Muses above the doors, and its mahogany floor into which is set the Queen's monogram; and next to that her bedroom, called the Chamber of the Five Marys, from its having been occupied by Maria de' Medici, Maria Theresa, the wife of Louis XIV, Marie Antoinette, Marie Louise, and Marie Amélie (it was also the chamber of the Empress Eugénie); then comes the music room, which used to be the Queen's card-room in the time of Marie Antoinette; and finally the Gallery of Diana.

All these rooms, like those of Napoleon's apartment, open on the Garden of Diana. On the ground-floor, beneath the Emperor's quarters, are the rooms in which used to live his mother and his sister Pauline, and the one used as his private library. As we have said, a narrow staircase, in which there is not space for two people to pass, connects this room with the Emperor's study above. It is in this library, crowded with books, that Napoleon spent most of his time after his abdication, searching in histories for sufferings that rivalled his own.

We will not speak of the sumptuous apartments that surrounded the Oval Courtyard, of the large reception-rooms of the last of the Valois, of the wonderful gallery of Henri II, decorated by Primaticcio, for they have nothing to do with the abdication and the leave-taking. The time for pompous ceremonies, for banquets, balls, and concerts had passed. Doubtless Napoleon recalled his former splendour, and his brilliant stay at Fontaineb-leau after the campaign of Wagram, when, as Cambacérès put it, he seemed to walk about in glory. He might have said to himself:

> Here I inflicted pain on my tender and devoted Josephine; here I dealt harshly with the Pope, that venerable man, who came to Paris from Rome for my coronation. I am punished for my sins. I recognize the hand of God in my chastisement. Had I not repudiated Josephine, she would now be by my side. I did wrong to imprison the Pope. He, not I, is free, and who knows if I may not soon be a prisoner?

At first Napoleon did not give way to gloomy thoughts. When he reached Fontainebleau, at six o'clock in the morning of March 31,1814, and walked in the gardens, he could not yet measure the depth of the abyss that opened before him. He had no suspicion of what threatened him. He never for a moment thought that his best officers—Berthier himself—would desert him; that henceforth Marie Louise would be only an Austrian; that he should never more see wife or son; that before the end of the month he should be obliged to disguise himself in an Austrian uniform to escape assassination at the hands of his own subjects !

From the time of Napoleon's arrival at Fontainebleau until his farewell to his guard,—that is to say, from the morning of March 31, 1814, until the afternoon of April 20,—he knew a succession of agonies which only a Shakespeare could describe. The outlook grew darker from hour to hour; from hour to hour he was summoned to make ever cruder sacrifices. At first, with no thought of abdicating, the Emperor hoped by a grand victory to drive the foreigners from Paris. Then his marshals, opposing him for the first time, refused to obey him, and compelled him to abdicate. He still thought to save his dynasty, and abdicated in favour of his son. It was an illusion!

He was compelled to abdicate again, and this abdication

included not only himself, but also his descendants. He—the Emperor—had to sign away with his own hands the rights of the King of Rome. He had one consolation at least,—that he did not set his signature opposite the clauses which he regarded as disgraceful.

"I abdicate," he exclaimed, "I abdicate; but I yield nothing!" Yet even this sad consolation was not left him. He was asked to sign a lamentable treaty granting his family and himself sums of money,—a treaty by which the Bonapartes received alms from their conquerors. This time the measure was full. The vanquished Titan could not endure this last humiliation; he abandoned the struggle and tried to escape from fate by taking poison. But here again he was disappointed; Death would have none of him; it required that he should live to bring it fresh harvests, to make one final hecatomb,—Waterloo! The tragedy which seemed ended still had terrible scenes before the curtain fell.

To return to the day of the Emperor's arrival at Fontainebleau, March 31: when he saw once more his palace, rich with memories of his happiness, where he had always been obeyed and respected, he really believed that his fortune had revived. That evening and the next morning soldiers began to arrive through Sens from Champagne, and through Essonnes appeared the vanguard of the troops who had left Paris. They formed around Fontainebleau, now become the Imperial headquarters.

All the way along, the soldiers were thinking of nothing but their Emperor. They said as they marched:

We fought for him till night. Let him show himself. If he is alive, let him tell us what he wants; we are ready to go on fighting! Let him lead us back to Paris! If he is dead, let us know it, and we will have vengeance!

Moncey, who commanded the National Guard of Paris; Lefebvre, who made the campaign, in spite of his sixty years; Ney, Macdonald, Oudinot, Berthier, who had just arrived from Troyes; Marmont and Mortier, who had left Paris, all reported at the Emperor's headquarters. Marmont established his own headquarters at Essonnes; Mortier, at Mennecy. The troops arriving from Paris assembled behind this line; those coming from Champagne took up an intermediate position towards Fontainebleau. The stores and the great artillery park moved towards Orléans.

The evening of April 1, Napoleon had, at different points, twenty-five or thirty thousand men. If his marshals, his generals, who had grown old in harness, felt weary, the privates, non-commissioned officers, and line officers were still full of ardour: the old ones set an example of intrepidity; the young ones, like their elders, thought of nothing but battles and glory. They felt like saying to their superiors who were spoiled by fortune and luxury, "You are tired; but we are not."

Could Napoleon despair, when hope still inspired so many of his men? With such soldiers under him, he could not endure to think that he was no longer the arbiter of Europe and the master of France. The thought of his wife and son in flight, of his capital in the hands of foreigners, of the Bourbons ruling in his place, seemed like a hideous nightmare. He was convinced that he was soon to enter the Tuileries in triumph; and as he looked upon his faithful men, he thought: With such soldiers, nothing is impossible. Today I am unlucky, but I shall have my revenge tomorrow.

He studied his maps and the reports of his troops with all the ardour of his youth, saying:

While I am here, the enemy is more fatigued than I. His generals, convinced of their safety, are scattered in the different hotels. The soldiers are wandering through the labyrinth of the streets of Paris. A sudden attack on the capital might have the best results. Why should I not try it? This is one of those crises, when the right and wrong use of minutes may save or lose a crown.

In Paris they are weaving plans against me. My way of meeting them is by a great military blow, a thunderbolt. The Allies have lost, in killed and wounded, about twelve thousand men, under the walls of Paris. They have now, I know, more than a hundred and eighty thousand men; I shall soon have seventy thousand. With an army like that, devoted to me, I can do anything. Already it calls upon me to advance; why should I hesitate? My luck has turned; the Allies have made blunders for which they will pay dear; they have been rash enough to divide into three bodies, one of eighty thousand men on the left bank of the Seine, between the Essonnes and Paris, another inside of the capital, a third outside of the city, on the other side of the Seine.

Their position is fatal for them if I know how to take advantage of it, and I do. I shall beat their three corps in turn. I am going to cross the Essonnes suddenly, and drive Schwarzenberg's eighty thousand men back into Paris, and make one last appeal to the patriotic heroism of the inhabitants of the city, and the tricolour will float in triumph over the Tuileries, on the Pavilion of the Clock; the traitors will return to their burrows; the peasants of Burgundy, Champagne, and Lorraine will complete my work by driving the Coalition across the Rhine.

Such were the plans that Napoleon was weaving at Fontainebleau, and it would be hard to say that they were mere illusions. Thiers did not think so:

> The opposing forces were very uneven, but the zeal of the army,—that, at least, in the ranks,—Napoleon's genius, and local conditions, might well have outweighed the numerical inferiority, and everything promised a fearful blow to either the capital or the Coalition. When we think of the prize of success, if Napoleon had triumphed, of France restored to its greatness,—and its true dimensions, not the mad ones, the Rhine frontier, not that of the Elbe,—we do not hesitate to say that the possible advantage justified the risk, even had all the splendour of Paris perished in the bloody struggle. The frontier of the Rhine was well worth all that might have been lost in the capital, and we could

not approve those who, after following Napoleon to Moscow, would not have followed him this time to Paris."

And the great historian adds:

If he was mistaken, it seems to us that it was better to be mistaken with him that day than to be mistaken with him at Wilna in 1812, at Dresden in 1813. Moreover, by overlooking the dangers of Paris, he reasoned about that city as the Russians reasoned about Moscow; and he thought no price too high to pay for the extermination of the enemy after they had penetrated to the heart of France.

Meanwhile time was pressing. A review was held before the Courtyard of the White Horse, April 1 and 2. Yet Napoleon did not advance; he was waiting for re-enforcements, and was averse to taking any decisive steps before he had seen the Duke of Vicenza, whom he had sent to Paris to try to treat with the Allies. Caulaincourt reported at Fontainebleau in the night of April 2, but he brought bad news. At noon, March 31, the Emperor of Russia and the King of Prussia had entered Paris, and cries in favour of the Bourbons had been heard as they rode along. White cockades had made their appearance. The Czar had taken up his quarters in the *rue* Saint Florentin, at the house of Talleyrand, which was the centre of Royalist intrigues.

The Senate had met April 1 with Talleyrand as President, and had appointed a provisional government composed of Talleyrand, Beurnonville, Jaucourt, Dalberg, and the Abbé de Montesquiou. Caulaincourt still thought that if Napoleon would abdicate without delay, there was a chance for the King of Rome. Alexander had received him as courteously as he had done when he represented at the Russian court the hero of Austerlitz and Friedland, and had given him some ground for this hope. The question of the Bourbons was not absolutely decided.

"Go back," the Czar had said; "make your master abdicate, and we will see. Everything proper and honourable will be done. I have not forgotten what is due a man so great and so unfortunate."

When the Duke of Vicenza reached Fontainebleau, he reported all this to the Emperor, and besought him to abdicate in favour of the King of Rome.

"You must not think," answered Napoleon, "that fortune has definitely decided. If I had my army, I should have attacked already, and all would have been over in two hours; for the enemy is in a most precarious position. What a glorious thing it would be to drive them out! What a glorious thing for the Parisians to repel the Cossacks and to give them over to the peasants of Burgundy and Lorraine, who would finish them! But it is only postponed; day after tomorrow I shall have the corps of Macdonald, Oudinot, and Gerard, and if they follow me, I shall change the state of affairs. The commanders are tired, but the men will march. My old guard will set the example, and not a soldier will hesitate to follow them. In a few hours, my dear Caulaincourt, all may be changed."

And he added:

No, all is not over yet. They try to get rid of me, because they know that I alone can alter our fortune. I do not care for the throne; of that you may be sure. I can become a citizen once more. You know my tastes. What do I ask for? A little bread, if I live; six feet of earth, if I die. It is true, I have loved and I still love glory, but mine is beyond the reach of human hands. If I want to command for a few days more, it is to restore our fortunes, to save France from her implacable enemies.

This interview, which took place in the Emperor's bedroom, lasted well into the night. At last Napoleon sent the Duke of Vicenza off to rest, and soon he was himself sleeping soundly.

The morning of April 3 he woke up still bent on fighting. So far from preparing to abdicate he was anxious to arouse the warlike ardour of his troops by a speech. In the course of the day he assembled his old guard in the courtyard of the White Horse and addressed them thus:

Officers, non-commissioned officers, and soldiers, the enemy have stolen three marches on us. They have entered Paris. I have offered the Emperor Alexander a peace bought by great sacrifices,—France with its old boundaries, thus renouncing our conquests, and losing all we have won since the Revolution. Not only has he refused; he has done more: yielding to the perfidious suggestions of the *émigrés* whose life I spared, whom I loaded with benefits, he has authorized them to wear the white cockade, which soon he will substitute for that of the nation. In a few days I shall attack Paris. I count on you.

Here the Emperor, who had been listened to in religious silence, stopped for a moment. Then resuming, still amid profound silence, he asked, "Am I right?" At once there was an enthusiastic cry of "Long live the Emperor! To Paris! To Paris!" Encouraged by their ardour, Napoleon went on:

We shall prove to them that the French nation rules in its own home; that if we have long been the masters abroad, we shall always be masters here, and that we are capable of defending our colours, our independence, and the integrity of our territory. Communicate these sentiments to the soldiers.

When the Emperor had finished, wild applause greeted him. The foot-soldiers waved their guns, the cavalry brandished their sabres, tears of rage and patriotism filled every eye. It was not mere enthusiasm, but a delirious fury that seized them. Patriotic joy lit up Napoleon's face, a moment before so gloomy; yet the very next day he was to abdicate!.

14

The First Abdication

Napoleon's soldiers were, like himself, still full of ardour. The troops whom he reviewed in the courtyard of the White Horse, April 3, passed before him at double-quick, shouting more energetically than ever: "Long live the Emperor!" An eye-witness has described the march of these valiant soldiers through the forest of Fontainebleau after the review; he says:

> At nightfall the serried and silent column moved towards Paris, marching with firm and resolute step through the Imperial forest. The venerable oaks, the mighty trees under which the veterans advanced towards almost certain death, the moonlight magnifying almost every object, lent a certain majestic solemnity to this warlike march. A sullen and threatening silence. prevailed in the ranks. Nothing was heard but the dull rolling of the cannon, the regular footfall of the men, the clatter of sabres and bayonets.
>
> The thoughts of these men who had escaped from so many battles were full of gloom. Occasionally they turned their eyes sadly on the batteries of howitzers that accompanied them. It was plain that they were deeply impressed by the oath they had just taken, and were solemnly preparing themselves either to die or to avenge the Emperor and the Empire, and to fall under the walls or beneath the blood-stained ruins of the capital.

While the men and non-commissioned officers and the line

officers were manifesting this heroism, it was far otherwise with the principal leaders, who made no effort to hide their desire for peace. In the immediate neighbourhood of the Emperor's bedroom, in the gallery of Francis I., they uttered their murmurs and lamentations. Whither does the Emperor design to take us? they asked. What can he hope for now? There is a limit to everything. Human force is not eternal. We have done enough; we must have peace. Have we not made enough sacrifices? Must Paris be burned like Moscow? Oh! that is too much. We must venture to tell the Emperor the truth. We must persuade him to abdicate in favour of his son.

What followed? By what process was the unhappy monarch compelled to abdicate at the very moment when he hoped to regain his fortune; when he was about to order the Imperial headquarters to be moved to a point between Ponthiéry and Essonnes; when he had just reviewed his faithful soldiers, and had uttered a most warlike speech to them; when he was planning a terrible revenge, to crush the Allies under the walls of Paris, to drive them into the Seine, and to scatter them beyond the Rhine?

Thiers and General de Ségur do not agree about the details of the scene which resulted in the Emperor's decision to abdicate. Thiers says it took place in the morning of April 4; the General says it was in the evening of the 3rd. We are inclined to think' that the story of General de Ségur is the more accurate. His account runs thus:

These facts, which I have received from eye-witnesses, explain why the Emperor, after his proclamation and the departure of his guard, so suddenly and completely altered his plan. They are, however, so important, that after writing them down, I read them several times to these witnesses in order to make sure of their complete and thorough accuracy. I should have preferred to say nothing about them, but that would have been an injustice not merely to the cause of truth, but also to Napoleon; it would have been adding to his misfortune the unjust accusation of an unseemly betrayal of himself and of our cause; of a faint-heartedness which history, in the absence of our revelations, would judge unfavourably, and which would unjustly stain his memory.

In a foot-note, he says:

Among other witnesses, I will cite Saint Aignan, Fain, and Marshal Moncey, who have often assured me of the exact truth of my account, which has also been confirmed by others. As for the part which Marshal Macdonald took in this abdication, it is from his own dictation that I have recorded all the particulars.' I have read them over to him, and he has pronounced them absolutely exact."

Let us then follow General de Ségur's account, which bears every mark of accuracy.

April 3, towards six in the evening, the officers met near the Emperor's apartment in the palace of Fontainebleau, to give utterance to their complaints and their wrath. Excited by all the violent remarks, which were like the beginning of those seditious military outbreaks of which the history of the Roman Empire is full, the violent and irascible Marshal Ney undertook to persuade the Emperor to abdicate.

He suddenly burst into the room of the monarch who was to reign but a few hours more. "Sire," he broke forth, "it is time to stop. Your position is that of a man on his deathbed. You must make your will and abdicate in favour of the King of Rome."

"But we can still fight. We can recover our fortune."

"No! that is impossible. The army will not follow you; you have lost its confidence."

"The army will be sufficiently obedient to punish you for your revolt."

"What! if you had the power, should I be here now?"

The marshal grew excited by his own words; his voice and gestures became threatening. Seeing that he had gone too far, he stopped, and added, more gently: "Don't be afraid; we haven't come here to act a Saint Petersburg scene before you." And in a few moments he withdrew in anything but a respectful attitude.

Napoleon knew that he was ruined. What! One of his lieutenants, a marshal, had dared to use such language to him, the Emperor! When men the day before so humble, so docile, presumed so far, all, he saw, must be in ruins, the last gleam of hope must have vanished. Illusion was impossible. Napoleon saw his fate before him. He knew that the next day he should be forced to abdicate. Then he wrote to the Baron de Méneval a letter in which he ordered him to urge Marie Louise to appeal to her father and Metternich to establish her right to the Regency, adding this sinister prophecy—that even this might fail, in which case everything, even death, would be possible, and there would then be nothing left for the Empress but to throw herself and her son into the arms of the Emperor of Austria.

The next day, April 4, at about eleven in the morning, Ney, Berthier, Caulaincourt, Moncey, Lefebvre, and the Duke of Bassano met in the Emperor's dining-room, and waited for him there. Soon he appeared. "Stay!" he said to them, without another word; he breakfasted hurriedly, and returned to his drawing-room, bidding them follow. They gathered about him in silence.

After meditating for a few moments, he looked at Caulaincourt, and exclaimed:

Well, since they refuse to treat with me, since my resistance would be the signal for civil war, I am willing to sacrifice myself for the happiness of France. I will abdicate.

At these words, Marshal Moncey seized the Emperor's hand, and kissing it respectfully, said: "Sire, you save France. Receive my tribute of admiration and gratitude."

Then, as Napoleon looked at him with some surprise, he added: "Do not misunderstand me, that is my feeling, Sire; but give the command, and I shall follow you wherever you please."

Then the Emperor called his secretary, Baron Fain, and asked him to bring the draft of the abdication. At Caulaincourt's suggestion, he made two changes with his own hand. "There it is," he said at last to Caulaincourt, "and so it shall stand. I shall make no further alterations."

Caulaincourt read the paper aloud; it ran thus:

The Allied Powers having declared that the Emperor Napoleon was the sole obstacle to the re-establishment of peace in Europe, the Emperor Napoleon, faithful to his oath, declares that he is ready to descend from the throne, to leave France, even to die, for the good of his country, inseparable from the rights of his son, from those of the Empress's Regency, and the maintenance of the laws of the Empire. Done at Fontainebleau, April 4, 1814.

When the reading was over, Marshal Oudinot, the Duke of Reggio, and Marshal Macdonald, Duke of Taranto, were announced. They had come from Champagne, a few hours in advance of their troops, who had made the campaign with the Emperor, following him in his march to the east and returning towards Paris, though in spite of every effort they had not been able to reach him in time to save the capital. At last the three corps of Oudinot, Macdonald, and Gerard were near Fontainebleau,—those three army corps which the Emperor longed for so ardently when he reached the Fountains of Juvisy, alone, the night of March 30, at the very moment when the capitulation of Paris was about to be signed! They were approaching, and if they were favourably disposed, and shared the feelings of the troops the Emperor had reviewed the previous day, the abdication just read might be a dead letter.

When he saw Macdonald, Napoleon asked him how he was. "Very well, Sire," answered the marshal, "but cruelly distressed and very unhappy because the fortune of arms has denied us the last honour of fighting before Paris and of dying in defending our capital from this great affront."

"Where are the troops?"

"They are arriving, Sire, but determined not to march against Paris. I come in their name to say this to you; I come to tell you that, however the capital may decide, not one of us will draw his sword against it, not one of us will moisten it with the blood of his compatriots."

"But I have never thought of such a thing. How could you think it?"

"Sire, that is what is said everywhere, and the army is united against it. They say there has been enough misery; they refuse to make Paris another Moscow."

"But what an odious supposition! what an absurdity! Do you forget my care and constant love for the capital? Do you forget all I have done for it?"

"But, Sire, does Your Majesty know all that is going on there?"

"Yes, I know that the Allies refuse to treat with me."

"That is not all; unfortunately this letter will tell you more."

Thereupon the marshal showed the Emperor a letter which he received from Beurnonville, one of the members of the Provisional Government. Instead of bearing the address: "Marshal Macdonald, Duke of Taranto," it bore this: "To Marshal Macdonald, Duke of Ragusa."

Macdonald had been given Marmont's title. Perhaps it was not an accidental mistake; possibly the writer had wanted both the marshals to read the letter. At any rate, that is what happened. Marmont received the letter first; he opened it and then forwarded it to his colleague. It announced the dethronement of the Emperor and his family, the recall of the Bourbons, the hope of the English constitution for France, the confirming of all the officers of the French army in their position. The Emperor took the letter, read it calmly, and then handing it to the Duke of Bassano, bade him read it aloud. This done, Napoleon exclaimed: "I sought the glory and happiness of France, but I have failed. I abdicate and withdraw."

"Oh, Sire!" answered Marshal Macdonald, "what a blow! I came to urge peace, not abdication."

"Yes," resumed the Emperor, "I decide to abdicate. But do you agree to receive my son as my successor, and to accept the

Regency of the Empress?"

They all expressed their assent by word and gesture.

Who were the plenipotentiaries to carry to the Allies this abdication, and to try a final effort to save, if not Napoleon, at least his dynasty? This is what Baron Fain says:

The Duke of Vicenza was preparing to carry the paper to Paris, and Napoleon appointed the Prince of Moskowa as his colleague: he wanted to add the Duke of Ragusa, the oldest of his fellow-soldiers surviving, feeling that in an affair of such vital importance for his family he needed such support as his old *aide* would give. This appointment was about to be made out when someone suggested to Napoleon that in a negotiation in which the army was concerned it would be well to employ a man like the Duke of Taranto, who would have more influence because he was less intimate with Napoleon.

The Duke of Bassano, when Napoleon asked his opinion, thought that whatever Marshal Macdonald's opinions might be, he was too honourable a man to act otherwise than with scrupulous rectitude in a matter of this sort. Napoleon at once appointed the Duke of Taranto his third plenipotentiary. But he still wanted the plenipotentiaries, as they passed through Essonnes, to tell the Duke of Ragusa what had happened, but to leave him free to decide whether he might riot be of more use in staying in command of his corps; if, however, he cared to take part in this mission to which he was appointed through Napoleon's special confidence in him, he would at once receive full power.

Macdonald prepared to leave at once for Paris, with Ney and Caulaincourt, and with Messrs. Rayneval and Rumigny, their secretaries, and he took leave of the Emperor; as he had his hand on the half-opened door, Napoleon exclaimed: "Come now, let us march tomorrow morning, and we will beat them again."

The marshal pretended not to hear, and bustled down the

Horseshoe Staircase, where he joined his companions, and drove off for Paris, to open the negotiations, the last and the only hope of the dynasty of the Bonapartes.

15

The Defection of Essonnes

Ney, Macdonald, and Caulaincourt, invested with full power by the Emperor, left Fontainebleau, April 4, 1814, to go to Paris to plead the cause of Marie Louise and of the King of Rome. They were to stop at Essonnes the same day to see Marshal Marmont and to ask the Prince of Würtemberg, the commander of the outposts of the Allies, for the safe conduct they required for crossing the enemy's lines and entering the capital.

Essonnes, a village in the department of Seine-et-Oise, four and a half miles from Corbeil, was the headquarters of Marshal Marmont, Duke of Ragusa, and of the Sixth Corps, which had been under his orders since the beginning of the campaign. The river issuing from the forest of Orleans, and falling into the Seine at Corbeil, is also named the Essonnes. This river separated Marmont's troops from those of the Allies, and Prince Schwarzenberg had his head-quarters at the castle of Petit Bourg, a little village two and a half miles from Corbeil.

The three plenipotentiaries reached Essonnes at about five in the evening, full of delight at the prospect of meeting Marmont, who had covered himself with glory during the whole campaign of France, and especially in the heroic battle of Paris. Marmont, the companion of Napoleon's boyhood, his fellow-student, the friend of his youth, the eye-witness of his first exploits, who seemed the most enthusiastic partisan and most ardent and chivalrous defender of the wife and son of his benefactor, surprised Ney, Macdonald, and Caulaincourt by his gloomy face and embarrassed air. What was the mystery? What had. happened? Naturally, Marmont had hesitated a little before confessing the truth. Something had happened which was to bring ruin to the Imperial dynasty: Marmont had betrayed the Empire.

The Duke of Ragusa himself, in his *Memoirs*, recounts the circumstances that led to this act so out of harmony with his character and glorious antecedents. The first suggestion of the step was made to him at an interview held in Paris at his house in the *rue du* Paradis Poissonnière, in the evening of March 30, 1814, a few hours after the battle, when he was preparing to arrange the clauses of the capitulation imposed upon the capital.

"I must describe," he says, "a conversation which took place at my house in the course of the evening; for it fairly represents my opinions at that time. A number of my friends had met there, and talk turned to the state of affairs and the way it might be bettered. The feeling seemed to be general that the fall of Napoleon was the only condition of safety. Then we talked about the Bourbons; their most earnest defender, the man who made the deepest impression on me, was M. Laffitte. He openly declared himself their supporter, and when I repeated the arguments addressed some time before to my brother-in-law, he replied: 'Well, Marshal, with written guarantees, with a political order that shall establish our rights, what is to be feared?' When I heard a man of the middle classes, a plain banker, express such an opinion, I thought that I heard the voice of the whole city of Paris."

The members of the Provisional Government had at once thought that they could do something with the Duke of Ragusa.

"Yet," says Thiers, "Marmont had not a traitor's soul—far from it. But he was vain, ambitious, weak, and unfortunately these qualities, in time of confusion, often lead to acts which posterity blames."

A M. de Montessny, who had been his *aide-de-camp* for many years, had left the army to go into business, and had come out warmly for the Bourbons. The members of the Provisional Government thought he would be an excellent emissary to attempt to bring over the marshal, and they sent him to Essonnes, where he arrived April 3, at about five in the afternoon. He was the bearer of a letter from Prince Schwarzenberg, which ran thus:—

Marshal: I have the honour of transmitting to Your Excellency, by a trusty person, all the papers and documents necessary to give Your Excellency information about what has occurred since Your Excellency left the capital, as well as an invitation from the members of the Provisional Government to enlist under the banners of the good French cause. I urge you, in the name of your country and of humanity, to consider these propositions which will put a stop to the shedding of the blood of the brave men you command.

Marmont speaks of his feelings on receiving from the hands of his former *aide-de-camp* Prince Schwarzenberg's message, the decree of the Senate pronouncing the dethronement of the Emperor, and many letters from important persons urging him to accept it.

"It would be hard," he says, "to describe the various feelings this news produced and the reflections it aroused. The deep agitation was the forerunner of the feelings that the memory of those great events never ceases to call forth. Having been so long devoted to Napoleon, the misfortunes overwhelming him awoke in me that old and warm affection which in other days had outweighed every other feeling, and yet my devotion to my country and the possibility of helping its condition and its fate, inspired me with a longing to save it from complete ruin. It is easy for a man of honour to do his duty when it lies clear before him, but it is hard to live at a time when one can and must ask, What is my duty? Such times I have seen in my own life. Thrice in my life have I had to face this problem. Happy are those who live under a regular government, and in such obscurity that they escape such trials! Let them not blame what they are too inexperienced to judge properly!"

The unfortunate marshal goes on:

However great my interest in Napoleon, I could not fail to see what harm he had done to France. He alone had dug the abyss into which we were falling. What efforts we had made, and I especially, to avoid plunging into it! The conviction of having done more than my duty in the campaign confirmed my opinion. I had worked harder than any of my colleagues, and displayed unremitting constancy and perseverance. Might not these great efforts, which had been continued so long as there was any chance of their doing good, make my score with Napoleon clean, and had I not fully paid what I owed him? Ought not the country to have its turn?

After M. de Montessny had gone, the marshal told Colonel Fabvier, the second officer of his staff, the message he had received from the Provisional Government, and asked him what answer he thought should be made to the proposition it contained. Fabvier, who at the moment happened to be standing beside a large exotic tree, answered, pointing at one of the strongest of its branches: "It seems to me that under other circumstances the answer ought to be that. However, it would be necessary to inform the Emperor of this melancholy attempt."

"That is what I shall do," answered Marmont, and then they sat down to the table, In the evening the marshal drew up his reply to the letter of Prince Schwarzenberg; it ran thus:—

Marshal: I have received the letter which Your Highness has done me the honour of writing to me, as well as all the papers enclosed. Public opinion has always been the rule of my conduct. The army and the people, being freed from their oath of fidelity to the Emperor Napoleon by the decree of the Senate, I am disposed to assist a union between the people and the army, which shall prevent all chance of civil war, and the effusion of French blood. Hence I am ready to leave, with my troops, the army of the Emperor Napoleon, on the following conditions, for which I desire a written guarantee:—

Article 1. I, Prince Schwarzenberg, Marshal and Commander-in-chief of the Allied Armies, do hereby guarantee to all the French troops, who in accordance with the decree of the Senate of April 2, shall leave the standard of Napoleon Bonaparte, that they shall be able freely to withdraw to Normandy, with arms, baggage, and supplies, and with all the military honours accorded to the Allied troops.

Article 2. That if, in consequence of this movement, the events of war should throw into the hands of the Allied Powers the person of Napoleon Bonaparte, his life and liberty shall be guaranteed him within some narrow territory in some limited region, to be chosen by the Allied Powers and the French Government.

The next day, April 4, Marmont summoned all his generals except General Chastel, to his room, and there drew a picture of the condition of things in connection with his plan. He said that the Emperor, after committing fault after fault, and having by his tactical blunders, let the Allies enter Paris, now entertained the mad idea of attacking them in Paris itself, with fifty thousand men against two hundred thousand, thus exposing the few soldiers left him to almost certain destruction beneath the ruins of the capital and of France. He then urged them to hand in their adhesion to the Provisional Government. Then he^ read to them his answer to Prince Schwarzenberg's letter, of which they approved both the matter and the manner, and Marmont at once sent it to the commander-in-chief.

A few moments later he thought of explaining himself to the

Emperor, for his conscience was beginning to trouble him. That same day, April 4, he wrote the following letter which, however, he did not send, for before night he became aware of the magnitude of the fault he had committed, and abandoned, though too late, his fatal decision:—

Essonnes, April 4, 1814. Sire: I have served you with devotion for more than twenty years, and my zeal has only been redoubled with your misfortunes. Sustained by the opinion of my country, my efforts would have had no limit, for adversity has never had terrors for me. But, Sire, it is against the opinion of France, and soon against Frenchmen themselves, that we turn our arms. The excitement prevailing in Paris, Lyons, Bordeaux, Marseilles, the unanimous feeling expressed with so much warmth, the decree of the Senate, indicate the true public opinion, and this should be the law for a good Frenchman, for a citizen. Moreover, Sire, in what a terrible position we are placed! Either fortune will temporarily crown your efforts, and then the sacking of Paris and the flight of its inhabitants are the result; or it is unfavourable, and then, Sire, with your immediate ruin is bound up the ruin of the rest of the militia, perhaps too soon necessary for the safety of the country, who, fighting for it supported by opinion, will be able to save it.

It is then out of devotion to France that I do what my heart condemns, but what is commanded by my country's welfare. I ought to withdraw from your ranks the day that the nation reproves you; but, after saving the country, I am ready to place my head at your disposal, if you desire it. I have not tampered with the generals or the troops of whom you have given me the command. They all agree with me that the will of the nation should be a law to them, and that now nothing makes this doubtful.

Marmont was already anxious, as his letter shows. His heart was beginning to condemn the resolution he had formed. Continually the grand figure of Napoleon haunted him, inspiring remorse which tortured his inmost soul all the rest of his life. Four days before he had visited Napoleon at Fontainebleau, and had been most cordially received by the Emperor.

"Our noble defence," he himself says, "had received his praise. He ordered me to make out a list of rewards for those brave soldiers who, up to the last, had with untiring devotion and courage maintained an unequal conflict."

And now, four days after this cordial interview with his master, his old fellow-soldier, his friend and benefactor, his sovereign, Marmont was abandoning him and making him over to his enemies.

Meanwhile Prince Schwarzenberg had hastened to send his answer to Essonnes.

"Marshal," he said, "I cannot give fitting expression to the satisfaction I feel on learning how readily you respond to the invitation of the Provisional Government to place yourself, in accordance with this month's decree, under the banners of the French cause. The distinguished services you have rendered your country are everywhere recognized, but you crown them all by restoring to their country the few who have escaped from the ambition of a single man. I beg of you to believe that I have especially appreciated the delicacy of the arrangement which you propose, and which I accept, concerning the person of Napoleon. Nothing better characterizes the noble generosity of the French, which especially distinguishes Your Excellency."

Matters were in this state when, April 4, towards five in the afternoon, Marmont found himself in presence of Ney, Macdonald, and Caulaincourt. As soon as they had informed him of the Emperor's abdication and of their mission, the scales fell from his eyes; he saw the full extent of his fault.

"This event," he says, speaking of the arrival of the three

plenipotentiaries at Essonnes, "changed the face of things. In my isolation, I had not been able to consult the other leaders of the army. I had sacrificed my affections for the good of my country, but a greater sacrifice than mine, that which Napoleon had made, had sanctioned it. Therewith, my design was carried out, and I had no longer need to immolate myself. My duty commanded me to join with my comrades. I should have been guilty if I had continued to act alone. Consequently, I informed the plenipotentiaries of my conferences with Schwarzenberg, adding that I at once broke off all personal negotiation, and should never separate from them. These gentlemen asked me to accompany them to Paris. Reflecting that, after what had happened, my joining them might have great weight, I eagerly consented. Before leaving Essonnes, I explained to the generals I left in command, among others to the oldest, General Souham, and to Generals Campons and Bordessoulle, the reasons for my absence, and announced to them my speedy return. I ordered them, in the presence of the plenipotentiaries, in no circumstances to make the slightest movement before my return."

Night had fallen when the three plenipotentiaries, accompanied by Marmont reached Petit Bourg, Prince Schwarzenberg's headquarters, to ask for the safe-conduct necessary for the continuation of their journey. At this moment Marmont felt extremely embarrassed; he wondered how he could explain his conduct to the man with whom he had made an agreement that morning. His fellow-travellers took pity on him, and after they had got out of their carriage, they covered him with their cloaks to prevent his being seen; then they entered the castle of Petit Bourg.

There they met first, the Prince of Würtemberg, who spoke of Napoleon in the bitterest terms. Ney had formerly had this German Prince under his orders and had never spared him. He said to him: "If there is a house in Europe that has no right to accuse the Emperor Napoleon of ambition, it is assuredly the house of Würtemberg." In fact, it was to the Emperor that the sovereign of this country owed his title of King, and it was to Napoleon's brother that he had given his daughter in marriage. Then Prince Schwarzenberg made his appearance, and while he treated the three plenipotentiaries most courteously, he manifested no interest in the regency of Marie Louise.

When he heard that Marshal Marmont was in the carriage below, he desired to have a private talk with him. "In this interview," says the marshal, "I released myself from' the arrangements we had made, explaining my motives to Prince Schwarzenberg. The change in the general position of affairs would naturally make one in my conduct. My acts had been inspired by a desire to save my country, and since a measure undertaken in common with my comrades, and in concert with Napoleon, promised to attain this end, I could not hold myself aloof from it.

He understood me perfectly, and gave complete approval to my plan."

Then Marmont joined his colleagues, and they all pushed on, with their safe conduct, and reaching Paris, April 5, at about 2 a.m., at once went to the residence of Talleyrand, in the rue Saint Florentin, where the Emperor Alexander was staying. All four, Ney, Macdonald, Caulaincourt, and Marmont, were immediately received by the Czar, who greeted them most courteously, saying that he had wanted to express to them the esteem and the admiration he felt for the bravery of the French army and for the skill of its commanders. He gave utterance to the most friendly feelings for France. "I desire," he added, "its happiness and security. It must be powerful and remain great."

Then the plenipotentiaries pleaded with conviction, eloquence, and energy the cause of Marie Louise and of the King of Rome. Marmont, who the day before had been a Royalist, became once more a Bonapartist, and added his voice to theirs.

> "I was not," he says in his *Memoirs*, "the least ardent in defending the rights of the son of Napoleon and of the Regent."

The discussion was long and hot. The Emperor ended it by saying that he could not settle this important question alone, but had to refer it to his allies, and that he could give no answer before the morning. The plenipotentiaries preserved some hopes when they took leave of the Czar; and the Royalists, who feared nothing so much as the maintenance of the Imperial dynasty, could not conceal their anxiety.

A fatal incident—a result of Marmont's conduct, though one for which he was not directly responsible—had just destroyed the last chances of the King of Rome, and made the restoration of the Bourbons inevitable. Marmont had merely planned the defection of Essonnes; his generals had just carried it out.

Scarcely had Marmont left Essonnes with the plenipotentiaries than an *aide-de-camp* of the Emperor, Colonel Gourgaud, arrived there in great haste. This officer had been ordered by Napoleon to go first to the headquarters of the Duke of Ragusa, at Essonnes, and then to the headquarters of the Duke of Treviso, at Mennecy, to tell the two marshals that the Emperor summoned them to Fontainebleau to receive instructions. Doubtless Napoleon, who had abdicated only conditionally,—that is to say, in case the allied sovereigns should recognize his son's rights, and who, moreover, knew that they had declared, on the 31st of March, that they would not treat with him or with any member of his family,—attached but little importance to the mission undertaken by the Prince of Moskowa and the Dukes of Taranto and Vicenza.

He believed that this mission had but few chances of being successful; and if, as was probable, it failed, he still hoped to march on Paris with his guard, and the army corps of the Dukes of Ragusa and Treviso, to make one last effort. Probably when he summoned the two marshals, it was to arrange with them his plans. Moreover, anticipating Marmont's possible departure to Paris with the three plenipotentiaries, he had sent word that if the Marshal had left Essonnes, the senior general of the Sixth Corps, General Souham, should report in his place at Fontainebleau.

When Colonel Gourgaud reached Essonnes with the Emperor's order, he expressed with some warmth his surprise at not finding Marmont. This made General Souham think that all was lost. He fancied that the Emperor had got wind of the negotiations that had taken place that morning between the marshal and the enemy; he recalled his warm adhesion to the proposed defection, and felt sure that Napoleon meant to punish him, possibly to have him shot. As a former officer of the army of the Rhine, and a friend of Moreau, General Souham had never loved the Emperor, and he feared him beyond all measure. It was this fear—most ungrounded; for Napoleon, who knew nothing of the events of the morning, had no cause for ill-feeling towards the general—that was the cause of the defection of Essonnes, and of the overthrow of the Empire.

When Colonel Gourgaud had pushed on to find Marshal Mortier at Mennecy, General Souham, instead of going to Fontainebleau, as he had been ordered to do, expressed his terrors to the other generals, inspired them with the same alarm, and persuaded them not to wait for Marmont's return before carrying out the agreement made with Prince Schwarzenberg, to cross the Essonnes and to place themselves and their troops under the orders of the Provisional Government. It was in vain that Colonel Fabvier entreated General Souham not to form such a plan; the only answer he got was: "It is better to kill the devil than to let him kill us." The generals called out their men, and sent word to the enemy lest they should be attacked on the way. The unhappy soldiers were ignorant of the reasons for this movement. All the previous negotiations about the defection had been carefully kept concealed from them. They imagined that their generals and the marshal himself were still faithful to the Emperor, and when in the middle of the night they left Essonnes in pitchy darkness, and moved towards Paris, they felt sure that they formed the vanguard of the Imperial army and were about to fight once more. Colonel Fabvier was not with them. Indignant with the conduct of his superiors, whom he had in vain tried to recall to their duty, he had just galloped away to find Marshal Marmont and tell him what was going on.

Meanwhile the soldiers began to form some notion of the part they were thus forced to play, and their suspicions grew at every step. When they saw the allied troops peaceably lining the road, letting them pass by without firing a shot, they were almost certain that some treachery was on foot. The scouts, who were Poles, exclaimed: "We are deceived; we are surrendered to the enemy. We will not betray the Emperor," and they refused to go. The rear-guard, commanded by General Chastel, had not reached the enemy's lines at sunrise. On seeing them, it suddenly turned back to Essonnes, and set about putting the bridge into a state of defence. General Lucotte's division, which was occupying Corbeil, had received orders to follow the movement of the Sixth Corps, but it did not stir: the general, in an order of the day, said that having been ordered to occupy Corbeil, he should remain at his post with his men. These, with the rear-guard commanded by General Chastel, were the only troops of the Sixth Corps who kept their position. The ill-fated movement went on. Some officers, who favoured the defection, invented a number of pretexts to deceive the men and to allay their suspicions, but there were murmurs throughout the column; already they had begun to speak of treason. When they reached Belle Epine, the troops left the road to Paris, to take that to Versailles, and it was plain that they would soon be in open revolt against their chiefs.

What was Marshal Marmont doing while his soldiers were thus deceived by their generals? After leaving Talleyrand's house in the middle of the night, he had gone to his own, in the rue du Paradis Poissonnière, to take a little rest before rejoining his colleagues in the morning at the house of the Prince of Moskowa, to return with them to the Emperor Alexander, before whom they were once more to plead the cause of Marie Louise and of the King of Rome. His conscience had been relieved of a heavy burden.

This defection, he said to himself, had been only a plan not put into execution, and he would do his duty to the end, vying in loyalty with Ney, Macdonald, and Caulaincourt, to save, if not Napoleon, at least the Imperial dynasty. Calm had at length taken possession of him, and he was sitting, buried in thought, before the fire, a mirror in front of him, his elbows on his knees, his head between his hands, when a door was suddenly opened. Then, raising his head, he saw in the glass the face of Colonel Fabvier, who was coming into the room. "What, you, Fabvier ?" exclaimed the marshal.

"Ah! I am lost."

"And disgraced too," replied the colonel.

"What is to be done?" asked the Duke of Ragusa.

"Hasten to your divisions, and stop the defection. Perhaps you still have time."

"Yes, yes, but first I have promised to go back to see the Emperor Alexander; come here in an hour with my horses and wait for me. I shall leave soon, and we will go together."

Marmont went at once to Marshal Ney's, finding there his colleagues about to leave for Talleyrand's residence, where the Czar had promised to receive them at nine o'clock. The Duke of Ragusa told them what his generals had done. "Oh! "he said, "I would give my arm, if only this news were not true!"

"Say your head," answered Marshal Ney, "and it would not be enough!"

When they reached Talleyrand's house, Marmont and his colleagues saw the enthusiastic delight of the Royalists, who regarded the defection of the Sixth Corps as the sure token of the restoration of the Bourbons. They knew that it would destroy the last scruples of the Emperor Alexander, and that now the chances of the King of Rome were irrevocably gone. They greeted Marmont as a benefactor and covered him with praise; they swore to him that Louis XVIII. would express his gratitude by magnificent rewards; they were rapturous with delight.

But suddenly their great joy was troubled: word came that at Versailles the Sixth Corps, convinced of the treachery of its commanders, was in open revolt. The Royalists were in consternation. The Emperor Alexander, who was but a cool supporter of the Bourbons, might perhaps say that the army remained faithful to Napoleon; the Royal ship might yet founder just outside of its port. Hence they surrounded Marmont and tried everything—prayers, promises, flattery—to decide him to put a stop to this outbreak, which filled them with terror and threatened to undo everything. Marmont let himself be persuaded, and started for Versailles. Just as he was leaving Talleyrand's house, he saw Colonel Fabvier, who had been waiting for him at the door more than an hour. The marshal was much upset by all he had been through, and he tried in vain to collect himself. His lips wore a pained smile.

"Thank you," he stammered to the colonel; "I have no need of you. It is all arranged; there is nothing more to do."

Meanwhile, the troops of the Sixth Corps had been in open revolt since reaching Versailles. Their generals, whom they denounced as traitors, had been compelled to flee for their lives. The colonels, after a brief deliberation, had thrown in their lot with the soldiers, and had determined to lead the troops to Rambouillet and thence to Fontainebleau, to place them once more under Napoleon's orders.

"I went to Versailles," Marmont said in his *Memoirs*, "to review my troops and to explain to them the new state of affairs; but hardly had I started, when news came of this revolt. The soldiers cried out that they were betrayed. The generals had fled, and the troops were preparing to return to Napoleon. They could not have marched two leagues without encountering an overwhelming force. I deemed it my duty to bring them back to discipline and obedience; in a word, to save them. I pushed on, and at every quarter of a league received most alarming messages. At last I reached the gate of Versailles and found all the generals assembled, but the army was on its march towards Rambouillet. When I had announced to the generals my intention of joining the troops, they. did their best to prevent me. General Compans said to me: 'Don't do it, Marshal; the men will fire at you.'

"'You may stay, gentlemen,' I said, 'if you care to do so. As for me, I am decided: either I am a dead man in an hour, or I shall have made my authority recognized.' Thereupon I followed the column at a certain distance. There were a great many drunken soldiers, and they had to be given time to recover their reason."

Then the marshal sent an *aide* to look at the troops. He reported on his return that they were no longer shouting, but marching in silence. Another officer was sent on to announce the marshal's speedy arrival. This filled the men with a false joy. They thought Marmont was still faithful to the Emperor, and when they saw him they imagined that he was coming to help them out of the plight into which their generals had brought them. They felt sure that the man hastening towards them was a friend of Napoleon.

A third *aide* carried orders from the marshal to his soldiers, commanding them to halt, and to the officers to assemble in detachments on the left of the corps.

"The order was obeyed," says Marmont, "and I arrived. I dismounted, and formed a circle of the officers of the first group I came to. I asked them how long they had been authorized to distrust me. I asked them if in times of privation I had not been the first to suffer, and in danger and peril the first to expose myself. I reminded them of what I had done for them, and of the many proofs of attachment I had given them. I spoke with emotion, with warmth, with feeling. It was said that an attempt had been made to surrender them, to get possession of their arms; but were not their honour and their safety as dear to me as my own honour and my own life? Were they not my dearly loved family? The hearts of these old comrades melted, and I saw many of these weather-beaten, scarred faces bedewed with tears. I was myself deeply moved."

In his *Memoirs* Marmont speaks of this incident as a great personal triumph. He says enthusiastically:

Oh, what power belongs to a chief worthy of his soldiers, after he has endured with them all the varying chances of war, and how clumsy he must be to lose it! I repeated my discourse before each group of officers, and told them to carry my words to the soldiers. The whole corps seized their arms, and, with shouts of 'Long live the Marshal! Long live the Duke of Ragusa!' started for the quarters I had assigned them near Mantes. It would be hard for me to express all the satisfaction I felt at this complete success. It was my own work, the result of the ascendancy which I had well earned over troops whose toils I had so long shared.

These poor, brave soldiers were deceived to the last. They were convinced that peace had been made, and that they were longer free to shed their blood in behalf of their Emperor. This, moreover, was made impossible. The Allies had just placed an impassable obstacle between the Sixth Corps and Fontainebleau. All was over.

Posterity has not shared the approbation which the Duke of Ragusa has expressed for himself in this matter. Thiers says: "It is not to be forgotten that Marmont was the recipient of Napoleon's personal confidence; that he was under arms, and held at Essonnes a post of very great importance. Now to abandon this position, with his whole army corps, in accordance with a secret convention with Prince Schwarzenberg, was not the choice of a free citizen between two forms of government; it was conduct like that of a soldier who deserts to the enemy. Marmont has pretended that he was guilty of only a part of this; and it is true that, after designing and beginning it, he stopped half-way in alarm. His generals, led by a groundless terror, took up the interrupted action, and finished it on their own account; but Marmont, by accepting what they had done, assumed the whole responsibility, and in the eyes of posterity must bear this burden."

General de Ségur, in his *Memoirs*, speaks thus of the affair:

A melancholy ending of a justly famous warrior! For Marmont possessed every quality,—a military bearing, nobility of soul, of manner, of face, a varied education, much intelligence, and an ardent imagination. Being always eager for glory, he heroically risked all that it brings, with the same contempt for danger that he showed twenty-two years earlier, when he had it all to earn with his sword. But pride, which was greater than his glory, proved his ruin. His fall was all the greater because he fell after the most heroic action of his life, possibly of the whole war.

When Marmont returned to Talleyrand's house, after allaying the insurrection, he became aware of what he had done by simply seeing who they were who' congratulated him: they were all the bitterest personal enemies of the Emperor. Bourrienne thus describes the ovation that welcomed the marshal:

> Fifteen years have passed, yet the scene is distinct before me. All had finished dinner; he sat down at a little round table in the middle of the hall, and there he was served. Every one of us went up to talk with him and compliment him. He was the hero of the day.

Alas, he paid dearly for his appearance as a hero! All these things were, in his words, "the source of keen anguish." Remorse tormented him as long as he lived. In vain did the Restoration heap honours on him. At the last moment he was the evil genius of the Bourbons, as he had been in 1814 of the Emperor. The days of July were no less lamentable than the defection of Essonnes. July 28, 1830, he saw once more the banker Laffitte, who had done him so much harm in the night of March 30, 1814; and Laffitte, under the pretext of stopping bloodshed, was to debauch the soldiers. And Marmont ruined the legitimist monarchy as he had ruined the Empire. Then, beaten by the Parisian insurrection, he arrived at Saint Cloud, and said to the unfortunate Charles X.:

> Sire, the battle is lost. A ball, fired at me, killed the horse

of one of my officers at my side. I am sorry it did not go through my head. Death would be preferable to what I have just seen.

And from the Duke of Angoulême he received bitterer reproaches than from Napoleon. He ended his stormy career in exile, and in the castle of Schönbrunn he gave lessons in strategy to another exile, a young man as ill-starred as himself, who had been the King of Rome, and later was merely the Duke of Reichstadt.

16

The Second Abdication

We left Napoleon at Fontainebleau, April 4, 1814, just when Ney, Macdonald, and Caulaincourt were leaving to take to Paris his conditional abdication. The Emperor, at that moment, seemed depressed and discouraged, but a night's good rest restored him, and when he awoke he was far from thinking that his career was finished. He hoped either that the plenipotentiaries would induce the Allies to accept his son's reigning, with Marie Louise as Regent, which would be at least a consolation, or that the Allies, by declining it, would thereby render his abdication null and void. In this second case, which was, perhaps, what he preferred, he expected to be able to resume the conflict. Imagining himself still covered by the line of the Essonnes, and by the army corps of Marmont and Mortier, and still counting on the devotion of those of Macdonald, Oudinot, and Gérard, he hoped to have time to receive the very desirable re-enforcements due from the armies of Lyons, of Italy, and of Spain.

It was in this state of mind that, in the morning of April 5, he was still forming plans of revenge. Hence it is easy to conceive of his grief and surprise when he got word of the defection of the Sixth Corps. All his plans were at once overthrown. General Chastel, when he drew back to the bridge of Essonnes, sent an officer to inform him of the disastrous decision of the other generals of Marmont's corps. At almost the same moment Napoleon received a draft of the agreement which this Marshal had concluded with Prince Schwarzenberg, and the Allies had speedily published. At first the Emperor refused to believe it. Marmont, the friend of his boyhood, his fellow-student, his *aide-de-camp* in the first Italian campaign, should have been the man to remain to the last faithful to his sovereign, to his friend! When at last he was obliged to yield to the evidence, Napoleon said only, "Ungrateful man; he will be unhappier than I!"

A clause of the agreement concluded between Marmont and Schwarzenberg spoke of confining the Emperor, if he should be captured, within certain limits, in a territory chosen by the Allies and the French government. This condition, the work of the plotter of the defection of Essonnes, insulted the Emperor both as commander-in-chief and as sovereign. The acceptance of such a favour from the hands of a man who had betrayed him, seemed the deepest of humiliations. This last drop filled the cup of bitterness to overflowing.

Napoleon had just read the resolutions of the Provisional Government and of the Senate; he was aware of the invectives, the denunciations, which dishonoured not him, but those who uttered them, and his heart was full. Abandoned by fortune, the hero of so many battles gathered himself together, and in an order of the day, addressed to his army, thus expressed his grief.

This paper, so full of dignified sorrow, begins with a calm reference to Marmont's conduct: "Fontainebleau, April 5, 1814. The Emperor thanks the army for the devotion it exhibits to him, and especially for recognizing that France is in him, and not in the people of the capital. The soldier follows the good or evil fortune of his general; his honour is his religion. The Duke of Ragusa has not inspired his fellow-soldiers with this feeling; he has gone over to the Allies. The Emperor cannot approve of the conditions under which he has taken this step; he cannot accept life and liberty from the mercy of a subject."

Napoleon went on to speak of the Senate, which had just voted his dethronement. Even Chateaubriand, the most eloquent of Royalists, has expressed his disgust with their cynical recantations:

Can one imagine the Emperor reading the official document at Fontainebleau? What must he have thought of what he had done, and of the men he had made his accomplices in the oppression of our liberties? When I published my pamphlet, *Bonaparte and the Bourbons,* could I have expected to see it expanded and turned into a decree of dethronement by the Senate? What prevented those legislators, in the days of prosperity, from detecting the evils of which they charged Napoleon with being the author, from seeing that the Constitution was violated? What zeal was suddenly seizing these mutes for the liberty of the press? How could those who had loaded Napoleon with honours on his return from the wars, now find that he had waged them only' in the interest of his unbounded ambition'? How could those who had ever supplied him with conscripts, now suddenly be moved by the fate of wounded soldiers, 'without aid, or nursing, or food'? When I ask what Napoleon at Fontainebleau thought of those resolutions of the Senate, his answer is already made.

And this answer is contained in the. order of the day of April 5, 1814, of which we have quoted the beginning.

"The Senate," Napoleon says, "has presumed to dispose of the government of France, forgetting that it owes to the Emperor the power it now abuses; that it is the Emperor who saved some of its members from the storms of the Revolution, and raised the rest from obscurity and protected them from the hatred of the nation. The Senate relies upon the articles of the Constitution to overthrow the Constitution itself; it does not blush to denounce the Emperor, without noticing that as the first body of the State, it has taken part in everything that has happened. It has gone so far as to dare to accuse the Emperor of altering its resolutions in their publication. "Everyone knows that he had no need of such devices. A sign was a command for the Senate, which always did more than was asked of it. The Emperor has always been open to remonstrances of his

Ministers, and in this circumstance expected of them the most unlimited justification of the measures he had taken. If enthusiasm has found expression in the public addresses and speeches, the Emperor has been deceived. But those who have used this language ought to blame themselves for the consequences of their flatteries. The Senate is not ashamed to speak of the libels published against foreign government, it forgets that they were prepared in its halls! So long as fortune smiled on their sovereign, these men were faithful, and no complaint was heard about the abuse of power."

After these calm, dignified words to the Senate, Napoleon thus closed the order of the day:

If the Emperor had despised men, as he has been charged with doing, the world would acknowledge that he has had good grounds for his contempt. He held position from God and the nation; they alone could deprive him of it; he has always looked upon it as a burden; and when he accepted it, it was under the conviction that he alone was able to carry it worthily. The happiness of France appeared to be bound up with the Emperor's destiny; now that fortune has abandoned him, nothing but the will of the nation could persuade him to remain longer on the throne. If he must regard himself as the last obstacle to peace, he gladly makes this last sacrifice to France. He has consequently sent the Prince of Moskowa and the Dukes of Vicenza and Taranto to Paris to open negotiations. The army may be sure that the Emperor's honour will never be in conflict with the happiness of France.

Meanwhile, the efforts of the three plenipotentiaries had come to nothing. After the defection of Essonnes, the allied sovereigns no longer felt obliged to be gentle towards Napoleon. So long as he had been at the head of fifty thousand men within one day's march of Paris, military considerations had outweighed many intrigues. Now that Fontainebleau was no longer a military position, on account of Marmont's conduct, the aspect of affairs was changed; the time for softness had passed; abdication in favour of the Regent and her son was no longer enough for a confident enemy, and the plenipotentiaries were told that Napoleon ought to renounce the throne, not merely for himself, but also for his dynasty.

Alexander clothed this declaration in noble and courteous language. When the plenipotentiaries told him that their instructions commanded them to treat only of the affairs of France and not of those concerning Napoleon personally, he exclaimed, "I esteem him all the more for that." Then he added that he had forgotten all his grievances; that his former friendship had revived at the sight of so much misfortune; that he deplored the necessity of sacrificing to the peace of Europe such heroism as Napoleon's, of reducing such greatness to impotence. He promised that Napoleon should preserve the title of Emperor and the honours due his rank.

He mentioned the island of Elba, indicating the possibility of Napoleon's securing the sovereignty of that island. All. this thoroughly disposed of the reign of Napoleon II., and of the regency of Marie Louise. The plenipotentiaries had to return to Fontainebleau for further instructions, and they had to lose no time, for from one hour to another Napoleon's situation was growing darker, while that of the Bourbons was growing lighter; and any consolations that there was still a chance of his obtaining grew more uncertain every moment.

In every quarter began to appear signs of desertion. As Baron Fain, the Emperor's devoted secretary says in his *Manuscript of 1814:*

The struggle has been too long; our energy is exhausted; everyone says openly, We have had enough. The only thought is to save what is left of our belongings after so many disasters. It is not weariness alone that has broken men's spirits. Every leader of importance has received from Paris conciliatory messages and separate promises of peace. The new revolution is looked upon as an amalgamation of all French interests, to which but one interest—that of Napoleon—will be sacrificed. Everyone, consequently, is hastening to Paris, where the new government welcomes all who abandon the old. Yet everyone is reluctant to be the first to desert Napoleon. But, they ask, why does he delay so long to leave his adherents free? There is much complaint about his delays, his indecision, and the desperate plans he is still forming.

"Since Napoleon's fortune changed," Baron Fain continues, "he is thought to commit nothing but blunders, and already new-fledged strategists are surprised that they have so long taken him for their master. Finally, little by little, everyone has chosen his party. One goes to Paris because he is summoned thither; another, because he must look after the interests of his branch of the service or of his corps; another, to get some money; still another, because his wife is ill. There is no lack of good reasons, and every man of the least importance who is not in Paris has some one there to represent him."

Soon the Palace of Fontainebleau was to be a mere solitude; the setting sun was at Fontainebleau, the rising sun at Paris.

When Ney, Macdonald, and Caulaincourt arrived in the evening of April 5 to inform the Emperor of the failure of their mission, they found him calm and dignified, blaming neither men nor things, nor yet confessing to despair. When they told him that the principal cause of the trouble was the conduct of the generals of the Sixth Corps, he answered calmly:

Doubtless, I decided them. I summoned Marmont; they imagined themselves discovered, and in their remorse, terror did the rest.

When he heard that that the allied sovereigns proposed to give Corsica or something else, he exclaimed:

Oh, Corsica, without doubt. They must have been afraid of the nickname, which they do not dare to pronounce, they have so long used it as an insult.

Their talk was brief. The Emperor asked if he should find in Elba an inhabitable house, and ordered competent officers sent out to find out about the island. Then he dismissed the two marshals, promising to inform them the next morning of his decision.

Marshal Ney, on leaving the Emperor, hastened to write to Talleyrand this letter, which was published in the *Moniteur*:—

> Fontainebleau, April 5, 11.30 p.m. My Lord: I went yesterday to Paris with the Marshal, the Duke of Taranto, and the Duke of Vicenza, invested with full powers to defend before His Majesty the Emperor the interests of the dynasty of the Emperor Napoleon. An unforeseen event having broken off the negotiations, which seemed to promise the happiest result, I saw that to save our beloved country from the awful evils of civil war, nothing was left to Frenchmen but to embrace fully the cause of our former king. Possessed by this feeling, I visited Napoleon this evening to express to him the wishes of the nation. The Emperor, convinced of the critical position in which he has placed France, of the impossibility of his saving it, appeared to be resigned and to consent to complete, unrestricted abdication. I am in hope that to-morrow morning he will hand me the formal and authentic document to this effect. I shall at once have the honour of calling on Your Most Serene Highness.

Napoleon spent the night of the 5th in reflection. He weighed from a military point of view the last chances that yet remained. He thought of Marshal Soult's fifty thousand men under the walls of Toulouse, of the fifteen thousand whom Marshal Suchet was bringing back from Catalonia, of the thirty thousand under Prince Eugene, of the fifteen thousand of Augereau's army thrown back on the Cévennes by the loss of Lyons, of the numerous garrisons on the frontier, of General Maison's army. He counted over what was left of the troops near Fontainebleau—

the army corps of Mortier, Oudinot, Macdonald, Gérard—and his faithful Imperial Guard, still devoted, heroic, and ardent. If all the marshals, all the generals, all the officers, shared the feelings of the guard, everything might be saved. But were there not germs of defection? Had not, too, the Allies established a sort of blockade about Fontainebleau, which was closing in every hour? Their troops were crowding every road.

A Russian army lay between Essonnes and Paris, another lay on the right bank of the Seine from Melun to Montereau. Other corps were marching towards Orléans and Chartres; still others were spreading out by the roads of Champagne and Burgundy, between the Yonne and the Loire. It was barely possible to withdraw to that river and there to organize a line of defence; but would not that be a signal for civil war? Would not France be divided into two camps under two flags? Would not the great Emperor be merely the head of a party? In spite of all these objections, he listened only to his own inclinations, to his warlike ardour, and wished to continue the struggle; but would he be followed?

All these thoughts tormented Napoleon throughout the night. When morning came, he summoned his marshals, and tried in vain to inspire them with his own energy. He spoke of retiring on the Loire. They argued that this would mean civil war. "Well," he answered; "since I must abandon the defence of France, does not Italy offer me a worthy retreat? Will you follow me there? Let us march to the Alps!" This proposition was greeted with perfect silence.

As Baron Fain, an eye-witness, says:

Oh! if Napoleon had only dashed from that room into the hall crowded with lower officers, he would have found young men eager to follow him! a few steps further, and he would have been received at the foot of the staircase by the cheers of his soldiers! Their enthusiasm would have restored his hopes! But Napoleon succumbed to the habits of his reign; he fancied that he would be lowering himself if he were to march without the high officers given him

169

by the crown; it seemed to him that General Bonaparte could not begin his career anew without the band of his old lieutenants; and he had just observed their silence.

At the Palace of Fontainebleau, in the Abdication Room, with its two windows looking out on the melancholy Garden of Diana, stands a little mahogany table which attracts more attention than all the sumptuous furniture around it. Imagine Napoleon seated before it, unable to make up his mind to sign the fatal paper without a final, heart-breaking effort. With one touch of the pen, to sweep away the colossal edifice of power and majesty! to wipe out the results of so many heroic sacrifices! Thus to finish the splendid drama! What! no more eagles, no tri-coloured flag, no Empire, no Empress, no King of Rome! Nothing, actually nothing, left!

It is easy to understand why, merely in writing the lines, his hand trembled as if palsied. Napoleon wrote merely the draft, of which Baron Fain made a copy, and this he signed. The original draft is in existence; it is barely legible, and looks as if written in cabalistic characters. There are two insertions; one consists of these words: "for himself and for his children," words that cost the unhappy father much anguish; the other: "faithful to his oath."

The document runs thus:

The Allied Powers having proclaimed that the Emperor was the sole obstacle to the re-establishment of peace in Europe, the Emperor, faithful to his oath, declares that he renounces for himself and for his children, the thrones of France and Italy, and that there is no sacrifice, even that of his life, which he is not ready to make for the interests of France.

What an agony it was for the unhappy sovereign to face those men, the sight of whom was a mute reproach; to stand before the honest Caulaincourt, whose excellent counsels he had not been wise enough to listen to; the marshals, who would remain in command of French army corps, while he, the Emperor, would perhaps no longer have a battalion under his orders!

What a torture for him whose slightest whim had been like the irrevocable decrees of Fate, to have to obey their repeated, almost insolent demands! And then to sign his own dethronement, in the palace where he had once been so splendidly powerful, within two steps from the throne! Napoleon stood up, cast one last glance at his lieutenants, and said:

You want repose; take it! Alas! you do not know what griefs and perils await you on your beds of down. A few years of this peace for which you pay so dear will do away with more of you than would the most desperate war.

Then sitting down again, he seized his pen and wrote his signature.

17

The Empress's Anguish

While Napoleon was abdicating at Fontainebleau, Marie Louise was at Blois, where she had been since April 2, though the government she had established there was but a mere phantom of power. Palm Sunday, April 3, the Empress received the authorities of the city, after mass; there were no speeches in view of the state of affairs, but the Empress, accompanied by her son, walked from one to another, with a few words to each, beginning with the clergy.

Her face was sad, although as one of the ladies present, the widow of General Durand, records, she was still in ignorance of all that had happened in Paris; the decision of the Provisional Government, the decree of the Senate, had not yet come to her ears; newspapers were kept from her; the Bourbons were never mentioned before her; hence she foresaw nothing worse than that Napoleon would be forced to make peace on such conditions as might be imposed upon him. She was very far from imagining that the Emperor of Austria desired to dethrone his son-in-law, and to deprive his grandson of a throne which seemed to await him.

The next day, the Empress had gloomier forebodings. We have said that in the evening of April 3, Napoleon, after the sort of altercation that he had had with Marshal Ney, which was one of the main causes of his abdicating the next day, had charged the Baron de Méneval, by a letter in cipher, to prepare Marie Louise to make use of her father and Metternich to confirm her rights to the Regency, adding that even this might fail; that in that case, anything, even his own death, might be possible, and that then there would be no other course left open to the Empress than to go with her son to throw herself into the arms of the Emperor of Austria.

This letter filled the faithful official with the keenest anxiety. Napoleon's allusion to his possible death seemed to foretell suicide, and matters must indeed be in a terrible state when a man of iron, like the Emperor, could use such language. M. de Méneval, without informing Marie Louise of all his fears, urged her to write a letter of entreaty to her father, and the Empress at once followed his advice. Von Helfert, in his admirable book about Marie Louise, prints this letter in German. It runs thus:—

Blois, April 4,1814. My dear Father: I send the Duke of Cadore to you to describe our wretched plight. I beg of you to be good enough to receive him. I have confided everything to him, and he can tell you better by word of mouth than I can write. Our position is so gloomy and alarming that my son and I have no other refuge than with you. I am sure that at this moment you alone can aid us. I am convinced that you will listen to my prayer and will refuse to sacrifice to England and Russia my peace and the interests of your grandson. I know that the Duke of Vicenza went to Paris in order to negotiate, and that the Emperor Alexander refused to receive him.

The Empress was mistaken, for the Czar had never refused to receive the Duke of Vicenza. She went on:

I am sure that in this critical position, the Emperor will make every sacrifice to give his people peace and rest. Paris would have been defended more seriously if it had not been thought that it was attacked by you and that you would not abandon your daughter and your grandson. Hence I entrust myself to your hand, dear father; I am sure that you will save us from this terrible situation. I send the

Duke of Cadore from my present refuge. My health suffers from all these trials; it becomes worse every day, and I am sure you would not wish me to live long in this cruel anxiety. Once more, take pity on me. I entrust to you the safety of what I hold dearest in the world, a son too young to know sorrow and grief. I hope soon to have to thank you for the happiness and peace which we shall owe to you. I kiss your hand and am your obedient daughter.

The Duke of Cadore started from Blois with this letter, April 4, and in his absence the post of Secretary to the Regency was filled by the Count of Montalivet. The Duke of Cadore, a former ambassador from France at Vienna, had been treated there with great kindness by the Emperor Francis, who had consented to be godfather to one of his children, and Marie Louise had thought that no one could better plead the cause of the King of Rome.

The unhappy Empress was a prey to the liveliest anguish. The Baron de Méneval, an eye-witness of her grief, thus describes her distress:

Marie Louise at times expressed her regret at having left Paris, and spoke of her desire to join the Emperor. The opposing obstacles, the conflicting opinions of her suite, caused her to postpone the meeting, which was ever in her thoughts. Her anxiety was intense; the violent emotions that had tormented her, her never-ending tears, her sleeplessness, had made her extremely nervous. She could form no notion of the passions agitating France. She continually recalled her father's assurances, and could not persuade herself that the Emperor of Austria would sacrifice her with her husband and her son.

Meanwhile, what was happening at Paris was about to shatter her illusion; she was in despair, but she clutched, like a drowning man, at her father's love as the only means of safety. "When she heard that the Emperor of Austria was not in Paris, she hoped that he would never give his consent to what had been done in his absence, and that his voice would be listened to.

At that time the Empress's attitude was above all blame. The Duke of Rovigo, the Minister of Police, who happened to be at Blois with her, thus unreservedly eulogizes her in his *Memoirs*:

The Empress was in the greatest distress. She was in tears during the whole week she spent at Blois; she had formed a wholly different opinion of the French. The malevolence of those who cast her from the throne has imputed to her lack of character, some of the misfortunes for which she was in no way to blame. If the Empress, instead of being a young woman under twenty-two, had been of an age at which confidence is reached by experience, and she had consented to listen to the advice of those in whom she trusted, things would probably have turned out very differently; but this was not the case: the Emperor had composed her suite, and she set the example of submission.
At home as in public she never neglected any of the rigorous rules imposed upon her youth, which made it impossible for her to have a private talk with anyone except her appointed counsellors. I had the homer of seeing her very often at this painful moment, and became convinced of her devotion to the Emperor. She said to me one day: 'Those who thought I should have stayed in Paris were right; my father's soldiers perhaps would not have driven me away. What must I think when I see him allowing all that?'

April 4, at 3 a.m., Joseph and Jerome, with the Duke of Feltre, Minister of War, left Blois, taking the road to Orléans, in order to ascertain whether it might not be well to establish the Regency there, where there would be easier communication with the Emperor. Joseph also meant to go to Fontainebleau, to receive his brother's direct instructions, but the fear of capture by the enemies' troops caused him to abandon this project.

A high officer of the Commissariat, who had been trying to rejoin Napoleon, had been prevented by the arrival of a corps of the enemy, and on his way back had stopped at Orléans, at the hotel where happened to be the Minister of War. This functionary invited him to call on him, and in the presence of a third person, who was no other than King Jerome, asked him the most minute questions, to ascertain if it was possible to make his way to Fontainebleau. The manifest danger caused Joseph to abandon the plan, so he returned to Blois with Jerome, and wrote to the Emperor this letter:—

Blois, April 6, 1814. Sire: I went to Orléans day before yesterday in order to see Your Majesty for a few moments. I could get no further, on account of the arrival of a hostile corps which cut off all communication. M. de Cadore continued his journey. We have had no letter since the 3rd. A messenger announces a suspension of hostilities. I hope it will be followed by peace.

Joseph and Jerome did not seem wholly discouraged. They had sent before them to Blois the papers of the Ministry of War, and forty clerks with orders to work night and day at recruiting. Communication with many divisions was still open. New levies were talked about, as well as organizing unattached corps in the departments occupied by the Allies. The Regency had sent to the prefects a circular in which recent events were thus described:—

The Emperor, who had transferred his head-quarters to Troyes, March 29, moved in forced marches through Sens towards his capital. His Majesty was at Fontainebleau, March 31; then he learned that the enemy, who had arrived twenty-four hours before the French army, occupied Paris, after a hot and bloody defence. The corps of the Dukes of Treviso and of Ragusa, and that of General Compans, which hastened to the defence of the capital, are united between Essonnes and Paris, where His Majesty has taken up his position with the whole army arriving from Troyes. The enemy's occupation of the capital is a sore grief to His Majesty's heart, but it is no cause for alarm; the presence of the Emperor with his army at the gates of Paris will restrain the enemy from their accustomed excesses, in so populous a city which it can only hold with great risk.

This optimistic proclamation was not published in Blois; for it was doubtless thought that it would not be received with favour in a town so near the scene of events. It was reserved for the remoter departments, and the prefects to whom it was sent were instructed to publish it with such comments as circumstances might make most suitable. These, for example, were the comments of the prefect of the department of Maine-et-Loire:

The Emperor is in good health, and watching over the safety of all. Her Majesty the Empress and the King of Rome are in safety. The Emperor's brothers, the high dignitaries, the Ministers, the Senate, and the Council of State are on the banks of the Loire, where the seat of the government is temporarily established. Hence the power of the government will not be paralyzed; good citizens, true Frenchmen, may be afflicted by the occupation of the capital, but they ought not to be alarmed; they should entrust to the Emperor's activity and to his genius the task of freeing us!

They should understand that in such a momentous occasion the national honour and a wise view of our interests command us to rally around our sovereign! Let us aid his efforts and spare no sacrifice to put an end to this terrible struggle against enemies who, not content with fighting our armies, have struck a deadlier blow at what every citizen holds most dear, and are ravaging this fair country, whose glory and prosperity have always been the object of their jealous hatred. In spite of the successes obtained by the Army of the Coalition, which it will not long enjoy, the scene of war is still remote from you; but if any marauders, led by hope of pillage, dare to appear in your territory, they will find you armed to defend your wives, your children, your property!

At Blois this patriotic language would have produced but little impression, because everyone there was discouraged. Wednesday, April 6, arrived the Polytechnic School, the School of Saint Cyr, and that of Charenton, and the pages. A pamphlet that appeared in 1814, entitled *The Regency at Blois, or the Last Moments of the Imperial Government,* contains this passage:

> The city of Blois was already full; every inhabitant had shared his house, his room, or even given up his bed to his new guests. These were polite, but there was dread of unpleasant ones, when it was proposed to establish two camps near Blois, and this news kept men's minds divided between the spectacle of the present and dread of the future, between surprise at the picture of the mutability of human affairs, as shown by this fugitive court, and the fear of an army which might be summoned to defend Blois, and might pay for its hospitality with all the horrors of war.

Meanwhile, Marie Louise, at the head of her dim shadow of a government, kept up, until April 7, a faint hope. She had been persuaded to sign a proclamation which was posted in Blois on the morning of that day; it ran thus:

> Frenchmen, the course of the war has put the capital in the hands of foreigners. The Emperor, who hastened to defend it, is at the head of his so often victorious armies. It is from the residence I have chosen and from the Emperor's Ministers that will be issued the only orders which you may obey. Every city in the enemy's power ceases to be free; every order issuing thence is the language of the foreigners, or of one whom it suits their views to spread abroad.
>
> You will remain faithful to your vows; you will listen to the voice of a princess entrusted to your fidelity, who glories in being a Frenchwoman, and in sharing the destinies

of the sovereign whom you have yourselves chosen. My son was less sure of your hearts in the days of our prosperity. His rights and his person are under your protection. [Signed] Marie Louise. [Countersigned] Montalivet, Secretary *pro tempore* of the Regency.

As the Baron de Méneval remarks, this proclamation, which was sent into every department which it could reach, and was the last official paper of the Regency, passed almost unnoticed. Since no one could foresee what might happen in twenty-four hours, the Ministers used to come to the palace in travelling-dress.

That day, April 7, Marie Louise, from whom her suite, moved either by pity or the habit of flattery, concealed the bad news, was still ignorant of everything that had happened since her departure. One of her ladies, the widow of General Durand, who had remained in Paris, secured a passport and left on the 6th, reaching Blois on the 7th. She gave the Empress not only the documents entrusted to her, but also the resolutions of the Provisional Government, and all the newspapers.

"The Empress," she says in her *Memoirs*, "had been kept in such complete ignorance that she could scarcely believe what she read. She was urged and entreated to return to Paris before a prince of the house of Bourbon should arrive; she was assured of the Regency for herself, and of the throne for her son, if she would consent; and her return would have been easy; for the lady who brought the despatches had travelled alone in a *post chaise*, with but one servant, and had riot been called upon once to show her passport."

For a moment Marie Louise thought of following Madame Durand's advice, but her suite dissuaded her from a decision which the Emperor had not commanded, and which doubtless would have been taken too late to be of any service.

The same day, April 7, Colonel Galbois, whom the Emperor had sent the day before from Fontainebleau, after making his way with great difficulty through the allied troops, presented himself before the Empress. He thus describes his mission:

> I reached Blois early; the Empress received me at once. The Emperor's abdication surprised her greatly. She could not believe that the allied sovereigns had the intention of dethroning the Emperor Napoleon. 'My father,' she said, 'would not allow it; he told me twenty times, when he placed me on the French throne, that he would always maintain me there, and my father is an honest man.' The Empress asked to be left alone to meditate on the Emperor's letter. Then I saw the King of Spain and the King of Westphalia. Joseph was deeply afflicted. Jerome was very violent against Napoleon. Marie Louise asked for me, and told me she wished to go to the Emperor. I told her this was impossible.
>
> Then Her Majesty asked me with some vivacity, 'Why so, Colonel? You can do it! My place is at the Emperor's side when he is so unhappy. I desire to go to him, and I shall be happy anywhere provided I am with him.' I told the Empress what difficulty I had had in getting to Blois, and how much harder it would be to make my way back. Indeed, it was a very perilous journey. It was only with difficulty that the Empress was induced to change her mind; but at last she decided to write.
>
> I was able to reach the Emperor without being stopped. He read Marie Louise's letter with the utmost eagerness, and seemed much touched by the interest she showed. The Empress spoke of the possibility of collecting a hundred and fifty thousand men. The Emperor read the passage aloud, and said to me: 'Yes; doubtless I could prolong the campaign, and possibly succeed; but I should start civil war in France, and that I will not do. Besides, I have signed my abdication, and I will not retract what I have done.'

It is certain that at this moment Marie Louise had no thought of abandoning Napoleon, but that she sincerely desired to join him. General de Ségur blames her for not doing this at once; and in his Memoirs expresses himself on this delicate subject:

> Madame de Luçay, my mother-in-law, a lady of the bedchamber to Marie Louise, was a model of conjugal affection. Twice in the Terror she had saved her husband's life by imperilling her own, with the most devoted and most intelligent courage. Being endowed with the amiable and attractive virtues, as well as with the notions of honour that distinguished the higher classes at the end of the eighteenth century, she had just secretly persuaded the Empress to go from Blois to Fontainebleau. Unfortunately, absolute secrecy was indispensable. Already the carriage that had been ordered was waiting for her at the foot of the staircase, when another person was announced, who had long had a most pernicious influence on Marie Louise's weak nature. The Empress, who was much upset by this unexpected visit, sent her lady of the bedchamber into the next room, and from there my mother-in-law could hear only too well with what perfidious art the generous and noble plan the Empress had just formed was changed into the saddest of desertions.

Our own impression is that the Empress's conduct at this moment deserves no blame. Not only Napoleon had not summoned her to his side; he was not anxious to see her. It would have pained him to have her see him at Fontainebleau, already almost deserted, with but a mockery of a court and a phantom of power left. Early in the year, in spite of his disasters, he was still a monarch at the Tuileries; he was the ruler of all France, and of France with natural frontiers. Now he was not even King of Fontainebleau; his Empire did not extend beyond the palace gate. He would have suffered at seeing the little King of Rome shorn of his magnificent heritage, and more for his wife and son than for himself.

He could appear in his humiliation before his generals, but to appear before the daughter of the German Caesars, the woman who so recently shared with him the proudest throne in the world, who had made so imposing an entry into the Tuileries only four years before, and there had lived amid unheard-of pomp and splendour,—that thought wrung his heart. Moreover, he was now contemplating suicide, which the presence of his wife would have made impossible. His secretary, Baron Fain, confesses this:

> Napoleon, who dreaded this interview, wished to remain free for the plan he was considering.

Meanwhile, Marie Louise's anxiety was telling on her health. She could not decide on what she ought to do. At one moment she felt sure that, in spite of all obstacles and arguments, it was her duty to go to her husband, even though he did not invite her; at the next, she imagined that it was better, not merely for her, but for her son, that she should go to her father, to plead, with all the eloquence she could command, the cause of what was left of the Empire.

She ceased to expect anything from her brothers-in-law, who cared for nothing but saving the fragments of their fortune; or from her councillors, most of whom had left her, while the others gave her uncertain and timid advice; or from the nation, whose defection filled her with wrath. She remembered the heroic cry of the Hungarians: *Moriamur pro rege nostro!* she had seen Austria loyal when its sovereign was unfortunate; she did not forget the attitude of her father's subjects after Wagram; the obsequious flattery of Napoleon in the days of his success was still fresh in her ears, and she was indignant with what she heard of Paris, and with the insults and the selfishness of the Senate, of whose members Chateaubriand said:

> The sordid effrontery of those Senators who, during the invasion of their country, never ceased to think of themselves, was striking, even when so important events were happening. The Provisional Government proscribed all the marks and emblems of Imperialism; if the Arc de Triomphe had been in existence, it would have been destroyed;

Mailhes, who was the first to vote for the death of Louis XVI., and Cambacérès, who first greeted Napoleon with the title of Emperor, hastened to express their allegiance to the Provisional Government.

All these apostasies plunged the Empress into despair.

While Marie Louise still possessed the means, and was yet uncertain of what she might afterwards be able to do, she desired to reward the fidelity of her household, and of the troops who had loved her. She distributed among them sums amounting to two hundred and ninety-eight thousand *francs*. Soon afterwards every one left her to seek their fortunes elsewhere, and thus, as M. de Méneval says, was dispersed in a few hours the Imperial household, which had been admired as an admirable organization.

April 8, Good Friday, between eight and nine in the morning, Joseph and Jerome suddenly appeared before the Empress and told her that Blois was no longer safe, that the allied troops were near, that at any moment she and her son might fall into their hands, and that consequently it was of the utmost importance to retreat from the Loire and establish the seat of government elsewhere. The carriages were ready, and they asked Marie Louise to take them at once with the King of Rome.

The Empress, still trusting in her father, from whom she expected a speedy reply to her letters, was anxious to place herself under his protection, hence she declined this invitation. When they insisted, she summoned M. de Bausset, to whom she said:

Of all the officers of the Emperor's household here, you are my oldest acquaintance, for I knew you at Braunau at the time of my marriage. I count on your devotion, and will tell you what is going on here. My two brothers and their archchancellor are there, in that room. They have just told me that I must leave Blois at once, and that if I resist, they will have me put into the carriage with my son.

"May I ask Your Majesty," he replied, "what is your wish?"
"I wish to remain here and to await the Emperor's instruc-

tions."

"If such is your desire, *Madame*, I venture to assure Your Majesty that all the officers of your household and of your guard will agree with me that we have to receive orders from you alone. I beg Your Majesty's permission to go and announce your intentions."

"Go, please, and then report to me."

The Empress, says the Baron de Méneval, was firm in her resolution not to leave Blois. Was her resistance due to her mistrust of her advisers, or to one thought which, in her agitation, completely controlled her? All that she had been through of late had completely upset her, and she could not bear to think of moving again and of facing the perils of a flight to which she could see no end.

Meanwhile, the first persons whom M. de Bausset met on leaving the Empress's room, were the Count d'Haussonville, Chamberlain, and General Caffarelli, the Emperor's *aide-de-camp*, the military commander of the palace.

"Still affected by what I had just heard," he says in his *Memoirs*, "I hastened to repeat it to them. 'That cannot be tolerated,' said the Count d'Haussonville, impetuously. With those words he hastened to the portico of the palace, where he fell down; but that did not prevent his shouting to all the officers of the guard who happened to be strolling and chatting in the courtyard while waiting for breakfast. They were at once aroused, and all agreed with us, and expressed a very warm desire to assure the Empress of their fidelity and devotion. I asked them for a few moments to inform the Empress of their wishes, and went into the inner rooms, asking Her Majesty to see me for an instant, and she kindly came at once. I told her what was going on, and prepared her for the reception of this manifestation.

"The Empress asked me to go back with her into the drawing-room, and I complied with her request. 'M. de Bausset,' she said, 'repeat to the Princes what you have just said to me.' I had the honour to tell the Empress that the officers of her household and those of her guard, having heard that it was intended to force, her to leave Blois against her will, had declared that they would resist this, since they took their orders from her alone. 'Repeat the words they used,' King Joseph said to me. 'We must know just what their feeling is.'

"'Their words would not be agreeable,' I replied; 'besides, the uproar in the next room will better convey them to Your Majesty.'

"The words were hardly out of my mouth when the drawing-room doors were noisily burst open, and all the officers expressed simultaneously and enthusiastically the feelings I had just announced in their name.

"'You must stay, *Madame*,' said Joseph, with great gentleness, turning towards the Empress. 'My proposition to Your Majesty seemed to me for your interest, but since you decide otherwise, I repeat, you must stay.' Everything resumed its usual tranquillity, and nothing more was said about her departure."

M. de Bausset adds these reflections:

Various motives have been ascribed to the Princes, who perhaps hoped to prolong an unequal contest or to secure more favourable conditions. It is at least certain that no one of us had approved the departure from Paris, and that we dreaded the consequences of a second flight. We were surrounded on all sides. Whither should we go? Capture was inevitable, hence it seemed best to succumb with dignity. In this circumstance the Empress acted alone, without consulting the Council, and according to her own feelings.

The drama was drawing to the end desired by some, feared by others. The same day, Good Friday, April 8, 1814, the Russian General Shouvaloff reached Blois at 2 p.m., and took up his quarters at the inn, *la Galère*. This officer, an aide of the

Emperor of Russia, was accompanied by the Baron de Saint Aignan, Napoleon's Master of the Horse, and brother-in-law of the Duke of Vicenza. General Shouvaloff's arrival was the signal for the departure of the principal personages who had followed the Empress to Blois. He announced the reason of his coming, which was to conduct Marie Louise and her son to Orléans.

Everyone went to the mayor's office for passports, which then had to be signed by the Russian General. The inn at which he was staying was crowded all day long. It was too small to hold the applicants, for everyone wanted to leave, and without delay. Those who could secure them, carried to the general letters of introduction; he said when he received them that he was full of regard for those who brought them; but, his time being so short, he begged them to wait or to come again.

"Most of the Ministers and Councillors of State," says the Baron de Méneval, "left for Paris. I saw the Minister of War, who, with his usual smile, told me that he had just bidden farewell to his former colleague (he had been the secretary of the Cabinet), and had given him a letter for the Emperor, in which he took leave of him: he added that when one left people, it should be done politely; that he had to give an account of the state of the war archives, of the store of maps, etc.; 'that he didn't want to pass for a thief.'"

The same day before dinner, the Empress summoned M. de Bausset, and said to him: "Do you want to do me another favour?"

"Command me, *Madame*; I am at your service."

"Well, you will start for Paris this evening. You will doubtless find my father there, and you will give him a letter I am going to write. I hope to go there too, for I ought and I wish to be with him. Make your preparations and come back at eight this evening for my despatches." M. de Bausset goes on:

I punctually observed the Empress's commands, and she gave me two letters. Then I went to Count Shouvaloff, whom I had known very well at Erfurt during the interview of 1808. I found his rooms filled with people waiting to get their passports signed for their return to Paris. It must be said the higher officials regarded their task as completed as soon as the Commissioner of the Allied Powers arrived, and thought themselves free to look after their private interests. Count Shouvaloff recognized me, and came up to me in a most friendly way.

We chatted together, and I told him the commands I had just received, asking him for a passport for Paris and thence to Fontainebleau, where I should await the Empress. The Count then said to me in a low tone, that the Empress was not going there, and that it was decided that she should go to Rambouillet when she left Orléans. I was about to withdraw, but I became myself a person of importance. Count Shouvaloff's amiability towards me made me the object of the warmest attention on the part of those who were most eager to leave.

The night of April 8 was spent by the Empress and her suite in preparing for the departure the next day. Early the next morning M. de Méneval called upon her and found her very uneasy about the journey. She had the crown diamonds brought to her, but she did not know what to do with them. She was aware that she would encounter bodies of Cossacks and feared that her carriages would be plundered, and was inclined to wear her jewels, being confident that her person would be respected.

There remained the Imperial sword, in which the famous *Regent* diamond had been set; the blade was in the way and M. de Méneval tried to break it off. Since he had no convenient tool, he broke it off on one of the andirons, hid the handle under his clothes and went back to his carriage, trembling for the safety of his precious burden. It was ten in the morning. Marie Louise, in company with her son, Kings Joseph and Jerome and their wives, as well as *Madame* Bonaparte, left Blois and took the road to Orléans. There she found a double row of spectators lining the way, who gazed at her in sullen silence.

18

Marie Louise At Orléans

When Marie Louise left Blois for Orleans, she was still escorted by cavalry of the Imperial Guard. The only disturbance on the way was in the outskirts of Beaugency, where the appearance of three hundred Cossacks caused some confusion. They plundered the last carriages, but the intervention of one of General Shouvaloff's *aides-de-camp* put a stop to the disorder, and everything that had been taken was returned.

On her arrival at Orleans, the Empress was still treated as a sovereign. She entered that city, Saturday, April 9, at 6 p.m., and was met by the civil and military authorities. The National Guard and the troops of the garrison lined both sides of the way from the city gate to the bishop's palace, where she lodged. She was greeted with cries of "Long live the Emperor and Empress!"

"I was filled with sadness," says the Duke of Rovigo, "when I saw the city of Orléans filled with troops; we had left still more at Blois, whither the supplies had been withdrawn from Versailles and Chartres. Why had not all these been added to the corps of Marshals Mortier and Marmont when they were defending Paris? No other reason can be given than that no one wished to do it; yet there were certainly more than twenty thousand men. Add to this number the arsenal of Paris, and it is plain that there was a lack of either head or heart, and that the Emperor was ill-served in this respect.

The city of Orléans was in a strange condition. After its gates were barricaded, its bridge manned, its walls equipped with artillery, it was suddenly crowded with the remains of the court, of the government, and of the army, with troops of every branch of the service who arrived without officers, and with officers who arrived without troops. The proclamation of the Empress Regent, signed at Blois, was still on the walls, but the Empire had vanished while the Monarchy had not yet come. There was a sort of interregnum which threw a cloud over the next day, Easter Sunday, April 10. The *Domine Salvum fac imperatorem* was not sung, but neither was the *Domine Salvum fac regem*.

After mass, the Empress received the Duke of Cadore, who, as we have said, had left Blois April 4, with a letter from Marie Louise for the Emperor of Austria, and who was on his way back. The Duke of Cadore had been able to find Emperor Francis at Chanceaux, near Dijon, whither he had been led by Napoleon's movement on Saint Dizier; he had not entered Paris with the Emperor of Russia and the King of Prussia. His daughter's hope that he could and would defend her and her son against the hostility of the two sovereigns of the north was vain, and the answer brought by the Duke of Cadore left her but little hope.

The Emperor Francis, while he asserted his goodwill and his paternal love, expressed the fear that his allies would not share his zeal for the rights and interests of his daughter. Marie Louise was then still devoted to her husband. As she was crossing a terrace which separated her rooms from those of the King of Rome, she suddenly went in and flung herself into the arms of Madame de Montesquiou, that clever and affectionate woman who was still the devoted governess of the Prince Imperial, and was all the more attached to the Empire because it was in distress.

Marie Louise knew that this woman would give only generous and noble advice. She encouraged her in her desire to join Napoleon at Fontainebleau as soon as possible, but urged her to await the arrival of M. de Bausset, who had gone on with letters for her husband and her father.

Then there occurred at Orléans an incident as painful for the

Empress as it was disgraceful for the Provisional Government. When Marie Louise left Paris, she took with her what was left of Napoleon's personal treasury, consisting of eighteen million *francs*, and gold and silver ware. There were, besides, the crown diamonds. Of these eighteen millions, what was left of the Emperor's personal savings, some millions had been sent to Fontainebleau to pay the troops or for the expenses of headquarters, and, by Napoleon's orders, Marie Louise had about two millions in her carriages, for her own use.

There remained about ten millions in the wagons of the fleeing court. The Provisional Government was in need of money, and it conceived the notion of taking possession of these treasures, under the pretext that they were the property of the state, which was absolutely not the case. For making this seizure there was chosen a personal enemy of the Emperor, M. Dudon, whom Napoleon had been obliged to expel from the Council of State.

M. Dudon, bearing an order from the Provisional Government dated April 9, went to Orleans and seized the treasures. Nothing was respected, neither the plate which was the Emperor's personal property, nor the snuff-boxes and diamond rings intended for presents. Napoleon's clothing and linen, even his pocket handkerchiefs marked with N and a crown, were taken. The emissary of the Provisional Government did not stop there; he seized the scanty silverware intended for the service of the Empress and of the King of Rome, not leaving one silver dish; so that it was necessary to borrow dishes and even china from the bishop in whose house the Empress was staying, for the two days she spent in the city. General Shouvaloff's *aide*, whose interference was solicited in vain, did not oppose the execution of the order.

The crown diamonds were given up with scrupulous exactness according to the inventory.

"There was lacking," said the Duke of Rovigo, "only the *Regent,* which was generally kept separate on account of its great value, and the ease with which it could be taken.

No one knew that the Empress was carrying in a workbag the handle of one of the Emperor's swords in which the precious jewel was set. When she was told what was going on, she at once took out the *Regent,* and gave it up. Her own private diamonds were with the others; she did not even ask whether they had been taken."

Easter Monday, April 11, the Empress again heard mass. Then she bade farewell to most of her suite, who were about to leave her forever. The parting was very sad. Marie Louise received each one in turn, and gave them presents of rings and jewellery, begging of them in touching language not to forget her. Her face was bathed with tears. A moment afterwards, all those who had left her came back into the room. They had heard that the Empress had been called to the throne of Parma, and they wanted to congratulate her! A final irony of fate!

The next day, Marie Louise was almost alone at Orléans. The bishop's residence bore no longer any likeness to a palace; only two or three ladies were left with her and the King of Rome. Cambacérès had not got so far as Orléans; at Blois he had taken the road to Paris, and without this customary adviser, the dethroned Empress was wholly under the influence of her maid of honour, the Duchess of Montebello, who desired nothing but tranquillity. Marie Louise's anxieties were boundless. The report that the Emperor wanted to kill himself came to her ears. M. Anatole de Montesquiou came to the palace on his way from Fontainebleau.

"Well," asked Madame de Montebello, "is it over? Is he dead?"

"Who, *Madame?* Of whose death are you speaking?"

"Why, of the Emperor's; it was said that he had killed himself."

"No, *Madame,* he is not dead; he is in the best of health; could you believe the reports spread by his enemies? Here is a letter he has charged me to hand to the Empress."

An active correspondence had sprung up between the Baron de Méneval, who was at Orléans with Marie Louise, and Baron

Fain, who was at Fontainebleau with Napoleon. M. Fain had sent word that every letter from him was dictated by Napoleon, from the first word to the last. A letter of April 10 said that according to letters received by the Emperor, Marie Louise seemed determined to go to see her father.

"But," it went on, "does the Empress know where her father is? Yesterday it was said that he was to be at Brie-Comte-Robert, and was to reach Paris today; all these statements are very vague. If you have more definite information, communicate it to us. The Emperor expects the Duke of Vicenza tonight, with a definite decision about his affairs. The Emperor desires you to ascertain the Empress's real wishes, and wants to know whether she prefers to follow the Emperor in all the vicissitudes of his evil fortune, or to retire, either into some state that shall be given her, or to her father with her son."

M. de Méneval replied that there was ground for fearing that the Empress was no longer free to go to the Emperor; this was her personal desire, he added, but she still trusted in her father's affection, who, she said, would never consent to her separation from her husband and son; she felt authorized by the Emperor's express desire to wait the result of her proposals to the Emperor of Austria. M. de Méneval said that the dread of being stopped on the way might put the Empress back, and that the idea of flight was repugnant to her.

In a letter dated April 11, 4 a.m., Baron Fain said:

M. de Metternich has arrived in Paris, but he seems no more favourably disposed than M. de Schwarzenberg. The Empress's plan to go to see her father seems consequently suitable to the Emperor; meanwhile, it is not known in Paris where the Emperor of Austria is. If the Empress knows, the Emperor wants her to tell him before she starts.

In another letter, dated noon, the same day, the Emperor made Baron Fain say:

It appears that arrangements were signed last night by

the Duke of Vicenza and the Ministers of Russia, Austria, and England; the island of Elba is given to the Emperor; Parma, Piacenza, and Guastalla to the Empress and the King of Rome. It would still be well for the Empress to continue to urge her father to let her have Tuscany, or, if that is impossible, to add to Parma and Piacenza, the territories of Lucca, Piombino, Massa di Carrare, and what is enclosed in Pontremoli; in this way the Empress would be in communication with Elba.

The Emperor's plan would be, when affairs are once settled, to go to Briare, where the Empress might join him, and from there they might continue their journey by Nevers, Moulins, and Mt. Cenis to Parma. The Empress and the King of Rome could rest at Parma, while the Emperor should go to Elba to make what preparations were necessary for the Empress's arrival. It is stipulated in the treaty that every Frenchman who shall follow shall preserve his rights as a Frenchman and his property, and shall be free to return.

The Emperor thinks the Empress should write to Madame de Bombers to find out whether she can come to look after the education of the King of Rome, since it appears that Madame de Montesquiou desires to return to Paris.

This statement was inexact: M. de Méneval told the Emperor that Madame de Montesquiou had never expressed any intention of returning to Paris, and that, whatever happened, she was determined never to leave her charge, unless he should be forcibly torn from her arms.

The letter went on:

The Empress will form her household anew at Parma and Piacenza, where there are many ladies of noble family. Since the Grand Marshal goes with the Emperor, Countess Bertrand will accompany the Empress. No one knows where the Emperor of Austria is; perhaps he will arrange to meet his daughter on her way. By following the route mentioned above, there will be no large cities to pass through except Lyons and Turin. In them she might sleep, and the Empress would soon be in her own territory. The Emperor is very well, and, as I have already told you, his health is not affected by his moral sufferings; he hopes to hear that the Empress is becoming consoled, and that she expects to be happy in the humble condition to which she is brought.

The Emperor is glad that the Empress is to have Parma and Piacenza, because her independence is thereby assured, and she will have the most beautiful country in the world to live in, if she grows tired of the rocks of Elba, while Elba is a retreat that can suit the Emperor alone, who no longer wishes to rule anywhere.

Affectionate as these letters were, they brought Marie Louise no consolation. The unhappy princess said to the Duke of Rovigo:

I am really to be pitied! Some advise me to go; others, to stay. I write to the Emperor, and he does not answer my questions. He tells me to write to my father; but what will my father say after he has let me be treated with such contumely? I am abandoned, and I commit myself to Providence. It advised me wisely when it counselled me to become a canoness. I should have done better not to come to this country.

Then she went on, her voice broken by sobs:

Go to the Emperor? But I can't go without my son, who is only safe with me. On the other hand, if the Emperor fears any attack on his life, which is very probable, and has to take to flight, the embarrassment I should cause him might make him fall into the hands of the enemy, who, I have no doubt, desire his death. I don't know what to do; I am broken-hearted.

Her face was covered with tears. Then she spoke of her father, whose abandonment of her was a cruel blow, and she said, with touching modesty:

I can understand that the people should hate me in this country. Yet I am not to blame. Why did my father marry me, if he nourished the plans he is carrying out?

Marie Louise's complaints were well grounded. Twice had her father sacrificed her to political exigencies: once in placing her on the throne, again in driving her from it. The gentle, peaceful young Empress was not born to face such tempests, and her character, so well adapted for tranquillity, lacked the energy and firmness necessary for supporting, without trembling, the burden of such a destiny.

19

The Attempt at Suicide

What had become of Napoleon since, on the 5th of April, 1814, he had signed his abdication, not merely for himself, but for his heirs? Remaining at Fontainebleau, he had fallen a prey to the deepest gloom. Being no longer either Emperor or commander-in-chief, he had had the bitter grief of handing over the command to Marshal Berthier, who gave in his allegiance to the Provisional Government. Like Charles V., he took part while alive in his own funeral rites, without having, like him, the satisfaction of seeing his own son reigning and his country victorious.

Passing suddenly from feverish activity to absolute quiet, this untiring man, to whom rest was torture, felt as if he were buried alive. His imagination was ever active; he already repented signing his abdication and wanted to withdraw it. False information led him to suppose that the Emperor of Austria regretted the haste with which the other sovereigns condemned Marie Louise and the King of Rome in favour of the Bourbons, and he still nourished a faint hope of some relief from the projected interview between the Empress and her father. He thought the abdication at least premature, and he blamed himself for it as for an act of weakness.

The diplomatic negotiations he had entrusted to his plenipotentiaries seemed to him humiliating and useless. Ought he, after enjoying such greatness, to live like a private person, and should the great sacrifice he had made for the world's peace be mixed up with pecuniary arrangements? "Of what use is a treaty," he asked himself, "when no one will settle with me the interests of France? The moment there is no longer any question about me, there is no need of a treaty. I am conquered; I yield to the force of arms. Only I ask not to be a prisoner of war, and to grant this, only a simple cartel is required."

The Emperor's face, once so glowing with genius and confidence in his good fortune, grew darker every hour. When for the first time in his life he was seen to be absolutely discouraged, it began to be wondered whether he might not be thinking of suicide in his despair. His pistols had been removed and unloaded by the Count of Turenne; and when the next day he asked for them impatiently, and complained that they were empty, it became clear that he had been wild enough to think of using them.

Napoleon appeared to have abandoned all thoughts of suicide when, in the morning of April 11, the Baron de Bausset arrived at Fontainebleau with a. letter from Marie Louise. As has been said, this prefect of the palace had been sent by the Empress, first to Paris to see the Emperor of Austria, and thence to Fontainebleau to give Napoleon the news. At Paris, M. de Bausset, not finding the Emperor Francis, had been compelled to see Prince Metternich in his stead, and he had been informed that Napoleon was to have the island of Elba, and Marie Louise the Duchy of Parma. As soon as he had heard this, M. de Bausset started for Fontainebleau and gave the Emperor Marie Louise's letter.

"Dear Louise!" said the Emperor, after he had read it. Then he inquired about the health of his wife and son.

"I found the Emperor calm, tranquil, and decided," says the Baron, in his *Memoirs*. "He had a well-tempered soul. Never, perhaps, did he seem greater. I spoke to him about the island of Elba. He knew beforehand that he was to be given this petty sovereignty. He even pointed out to me a little geography with statistics giving him all the information he desired on this place. 'The air is healthy,' he said, 'and the people are kindly. I shall not be too badly off there, and I hope that Marie Louise will find it comfortable.' He knew all the obstacles in the way of their meeting at Fontainebleau, but he hoped that once in possession of the Duchy of Parma, the Empress would be permitted to go with her son to live with him on the island of Elba. He was deceived! Never again was he to see these objects of his affection."

At about two that afternoon, Napoleon was walking on the terrace by the side of the Gallery of Francis I., at the end of the Courtyard of the Fountain, when he sent for M. de Bausset and began to talk with him about recent events. He was far from approving of the way the Empress had been persuaded to leave Paris, when the Baron reminded him of his letter to King Joseph.

Circumstances had altered, and required to be met differently. The mere presence of Louise in Paris would have been enough to prevent the treachery and defection of some of my troops. I should still be at the head of a formidable army, with which I should have compelled the enemy to leave Paris and to sign an honourable peace.

Baron de Bausset then ventured to say that he regretted that the Emperor had not been willing to sign this peace at Châtillon.

"I never believed in the enemy's good faith," replied Napoleon. "Every day there were new demands, new conditions; they did not want peace, and then I had told France that I should never consent to any condition which I thought humiliating, even with the enemy on the heights of Montmartre."

When the Baron respectfully suggested that France, even shorn as it was, yet was one of the finest kingdoms of the world, Napoleon said proudly: "I abdicate and cede nothing." Then he added:

See what fate is! At the battle of Arcis-sur-Aube, I did all I could to meet a glorious death, disputing the soil of my country inch by inch. I exposed myself incessantly. The bullets rained about me; my clothes were torn by them, and not one could touch me. For me to die by my own hands would be cowardice. Suicide does not agree with my principles or the rank I hold on the world's stage. I am a man condemned to live.

Then Napoleon, still followed by the Baron de Bausset, walked up and down the terrace several times, in a deep, gloomy silence; this he broke by saying with a bitter smile, "Between ourselves, they say that a living gudgeon is better than a dead Emperor." Then he returned to his room alone. M. de Bausset was never to see him again.

The next day, April 12, Macdonald, Caulaincourt, and Shouvaloff, an *aide-de-camp* of the Emperor Alexander, arrived at Fontainebleau with the treaty which had been concluded and signed the day before. "Are you bringing me back my abdication at last?" asked Napoleon when he saw Caulaincourt, who replied that the fundamental basis of the treaty had naturally been the abdication, and that had already been officially published.

"What do I care for this treaty? "resumed Napoleon. "I don't want to recognize it; I don't want to sign it; I shall not sign it." Caulaincourt carefully abstained from any discussion with the fallen Emperor, and let him sleep upon it.

The first article of the treaty contained the abdication; the second granted to Napoleon and Marie Louise the titles of Emperor and Empress; the third confided to Napoleon sovereignty over the island of Elba; and the fifth that of the Duchies of Parma, Vicenza, and Guastalla to Marie Louise with the right of succession to her son.

There were, besides, many pecuniary stipulations: an annual payment of two million *francs* to Napoleon; one million to Josephine; three hundred thousand to his mother; five hundred thousand to King Joseph; two hundred thousand to Louis; four hundred thousand to Queen Hortense and her children; three hundred thousand to Princess Pauline. Two millions were placed at the Emperor's disposal for gifts, a sort of legacy to be granted during the testator's lifetime. The treaty also permitted Napoleon to take with him and to keep as his guard four hundred volunteers, officers, non-commissioned officers, and men.

This treaty of April 11, which the Allies regarded as the height of generosity, seemed to Napoleon the lowest depth of humiliation. After signing the treaties of Campo Formio, of Lunéville, of Vienna, of Tilsit, of Presburg, to have to put his name to this miserable paper; after possessing an empire vaster than Charlemagne, to have to content himself with the ridiculous sovereignty of Elba; after leading the largest armies in the world, to command a petty battalion of four hundred; to have to accept alms from his conquerors for himself and his people, was a bitter and torturing disgrace.

Then to leave France smaller than he had found it; to lose not only all the conquests of the Empire, but also those of the Republic; to have even the tricolored flag abolished,—all these things were cruel! And then to have to sign such a treaty at the very moment when the Count d'Artois, the brother of Louis XVI., was entering the Tuileries in triumph !

Napoleon thought that death, that suicide, was preferable to the shame of signing so terrible and so disgraceful a treaty. At about six in the afternoon, in his talk, he brought up some of the memorable deaths, by their own hands, of the great men of antiquity in similar circumstances, and thus aroused the apprehensions of those who heard him. However, he went to bed quietly at about ten o'clock, and fell asleep.

About midnight he called Hubert, his valet, who used to sleep in front of his door. "Come, Hubert," he said gently, "let us have a little fire," and the two men built it up again. Then Napoleon bade his valet to go to rest. Then, after writing a few words on a piece of paper, which he crumpled, tore up, and threw in the fire, he went to the bureau and opened a dressing-case, in which was a little black bag.

Napoleon had worn that bag during the retreat from Russia

after the battle of Malo Jaroslavitz. When the sudden attack of the Cossacks took place, in which he narrowly escaped being taken prisoner, he determined always to carry poison about him, that he might not fall into the enemy's hands alive. Hence he had ordered Yvan, his surgeon, to put into the bag a poison formerly mentioned by Cabanis, the same which Condorcet had killed himself with.

This poison the Emperor took, to escape his troubles, in the night of April 12, when in the deepest despair. Hubert, who was watching him through the crack of the door, saw his master put something into a glass of water, drink it, and go back to bed. Since, however, he knew nothing about the existence of any poison, he fancied that Napoleon was drinking nothing but a glass of sugar and water. Still, he felt anxious, and listened for nearly half an hour.

Napoleon was surprised to be still living. Instead of dying at once, as he expected, he was seized with spasms, and suffered frightfully. He sent for Dr. Yvan, doubtless to ask for another dose to hasten the death he longed for. Then Hubert, still more uneasy, heard a violent quarrel between the Emperor and his surgeon. Yvan firmly and indignantly refused to be an accomplice to the suicide.

"You would," he cried, "make me seem a poisoner, an assassin, in the pay of your enemies. No! I will not do it!" The Emperor, who had caused the death of so many men, could not compass his own. Yvan gave him emetics, and then, still afraid that his patient might die, and distracted by the thought that he might himself be charged with murder, he lost his head, rushed from the room, ran down the stairs to the courtyard; there he found a horse fastened to the gate; he sprang on its back and galloped away.

Meanwhile, the silence of the long corridors of the palace was broken by much coming and going; servants swarmed on the staircases; candles were lit. Grand Marshal Bertrand, the Duke of Vicenza, the Duke of Bassano, were aroused, and they hastened to the Emperor's bedroom. "Everything has betrayed me," he "said to them; "I am condemned to go on living." Then he fell into a stupor which lasted several hours.

"God did not permit Napoleon to triumph," says M. Veuillot; "he deigned to punish him. God did not wish that he should satiate himself with success, like those men from whom an avenging prosperity expels any thought of remorse. He punished him, making him descend, perhaps I should better say rise, to the human conditions; he woke him from the intoxication of fortune, from forgetfulness of the last hour, and gave him time for the final battle, in which every man meets face to face the only enemy by whom it is important not to be definitely conquered."

To have died before the expiation of Saint Helena would have been for Napoleon the renunciation of the noblest crown,—that of martyrdom. The great man needed the purification of long sufferings. For his soul, so long the slave of passions, to become free, his body had to be captive. If we look at things from the Christian's standpoint, thinking of eternity, it was his jailors who were to be his liberators. At Fontainebleau he had not been defeated enough. He had not drunk the bitter chalice to the dregs. He needed one more final defeat,—that of Waterloo. He needed meditation and remorse on the wave-beaten rocks. He needed the dialogue between his stormy thought and the murmur of the ocean.

There it was that he at last was to attain real greatness, where he was to deserve a glance from the God of pity; there that, after enduring nobly one of the most pathetic and grand expiations known to history, he was to utter those ever-memorable words: "Not everyone who wishes can be an atheist."

20

The Last Week at Fontainebleau

Napoleon became reconciled to living. When he awoke in the morning of April 13, he was ashamed of having wished to kill himself, and bade his people maintain an absolute silence about the attempt. A violent perspiration, and some hours of sleep, had carried him through the crisis, but he was still weak and dejected.

At ten in the morning, when Macdonald called to pay his respects, he was seated by the fire, with his head sunk in his hands, which wholly covered his face. He remained in that position, without speaking or moving, for half an hour; at last he noticed that the marshal was there. "I am grateful to you," he said, "for the trouble you have taken about my last interests, and I am sorry that I can express my gratitude by words alone."

"In no case," answered Macdonald, "should I have accepted any other reward. Trouble of that sort is its own reward."

"Well," said the Emperor, "I am going to offer you a proof of my gratitude which even your delicacy will not refuse."

Then he had a Turkish sabre brought, which he gave to the marshal, saying, "This is Murad Bey's sabre. I won it at the battle of Mount Tabor. It shall be a souvenir from me to you."

Napoleon's face, which in the morning had been of a ghastly pallor, regained colour during the day. He grew completely calm, and affixed his signature to the treaty which, the night before, had filled him with such mortal anguish. "God does not want me to die," he said, and complete resignation succeeded to his previous agitation. Possibly a ray of hope arose within him; possibly he thought that the Allies were very imprudent in giving him a residence so near his former Empire; possibly he foresaw the blunders of the Bourbons, and his own triumphal return to the Tuileries.

However, in April, 1814, such a dream would have seemed most improbable. Never was a fallen sovereign pursued with bitterer insults and curses than Napoleon. With a few noble exceptions, all his old servitors left him. Berthier, on whom he had heaped so many favours; Berthier, his major-general, his intimate, with whom he shared his tent, left Fontainebleau promising to be back the next day.

"He won't come back," the Emperor said coldly to the Duke of Bassano.

"What, Sire, this is Berthier's farewell?"

"Yes; I tell you he won't come back."

Every moment there was a new departure; one left on account of his health; another, for some family reason; every one promised to return, but no one appeared again. Fontainebleau had become a waste, a city of the dead; and Napoleon, gloomy, silent, and solitary, bore more likeness to a monk in a cloister than to a sovereign, in a palace.

"Napoleon already is nothing but a common man," says Baron Fain, who witnessed his hours of despondency. "He lives retired in a corner of the palace. If he leaves his room for a few minutes, it is to walk in the little garden (the Garden of Diana). Whenever he hears a carriage drive into the courtyard, he asks if it is not Berthier coming back, or one of his former ministers come to take leave. He expects to see Molé, Fontanes, and the many others' who owe him a last expression of devotion; but no one comes."

When he went back to his room, Napoleon used to read all the Paris newspapers, which were full of venomous hatred. Their frantic attacks, the storm of insult and abuse, did not move him; and when their inventions became absurd, he would only smile.

The devotion of the brave soldiers who remained faithful consoled him for the many apostasies. They used to walk about the walls and gardens of. the palace trying to see through the railings the man whom they still idolized. When he was strolling in the Garden of Diana, they at every moment brought up non-commissioned officers and men of the Imperial Guard who begged to be allowed to join his battalion; and they who had never asked for reward or promotion now asked for exile. Lamartine says:

> Great affections come from the masses, because they come from nature. Nature is magnanimous; courts are selfish; favour corrupts.

There were in the higher ranks some noble examples of disinterested attachment. There was the Duke of Vicenza, who, with his usual energy, was making all the preparations for departure as if he were still Grand Master of the Horse; and the Duke of Bassano, of whom Baron Fain says:

> He never leaves Napoleon for a moment. The Emperor, when he opens his heart to this Minister, in whom he has the utmost confidence, shows the same inward serenity that used to appear on his face in his happiest days. To see this Minister's manners, one would never believe that those days are gone; there is the same simplicity in his attentions and consideration. Duty and love are manifest in them; and if they sometimes become touching and almost formal, it is because they come from a brave and sympathetic nature.

Napoleon was always touched by the zealous affections of this loyal servant.

"Bassano," he said to him, "they say you prevented my making peace. What do you say to that? This charge ought to make you smile, like those they bring against me nowadays."

General Bertrand, who was to discharge the duties of Grand Marshal of the Palace, not merely at Elba, but also at Saint

Helena, stands forth as a living image of fidelity. As for General Drouot, the Sage of the Grand Army, as Napoleon used to call him, he was to immortalize himself by his devotion to his unhappy sovereign. Lacordaire, in his funeral oration on this eminently virtuous man, said:

> The fall of the Empire, by setting General Drouot face to face with misfortune, has left him famous in a rare way. He loved the Empire and the Emperor with a chivalrous affection: the Empire, because he thought it the highest pitch of greatness which France had attained since Charlemagne; the Emperor, because he spent with him two years of suffering and defeat, and had perceived the man's heart under the monarch's trappings and the conqueror's pride. The fall of those two giants, the Emperor and the Empire, was for him a blow which we can scarcely comprehend, so remote are we from the events, and acquainted with them only through reading the pallid story on the cold, and often heartless, page. But those who put into that magnificent work twenty years of their toil and of their hearts' blood, those who grew old on the battle-field between glory and death, ever present and ever mingling, and who, in raising France, believed that they served a patriotic and just cause, they must have known, when their work crumbled, an anguish which we can neither describe nor feel.

General Drouot was to be the governor of this island of Elba. At Fontainebleau, a few days before they started thither, Napoleon asked the General how rich he was, and when he answered that he had about two thousand five hundred *francs* a year, Napoleon said, "That is too little; no one knows what may happen. I don't want you to come to want after my time; I am going to give you two hundred thousand *francs*."

Drouot declined them; but seeing that the Emperor was pained, he said:

> If Your Majesty were to give me the money now, people would say that the Emperor Napoleon, in adversity, had

only friends whom he bought, and that I followed Your Majesty because I was paid for so doing.

Drouot reminds us of Shakespeare's words:—

Yet he that can endure
To follow with allegiance a fall'n lord
Does conquer him that did his master conquer.
(Antony and Cleopatra, Act 3., sc. 13.)

Napoleon was more and more touched by the marks of devotion he received from so many officers and men.

He received Colonel de Montholon, who had just been making a reconnoissance on the upper Loire, and who told him that he could count on the people of the South and collect their troops. "It is too late," answered Napoleon; "that now would mean civil war, and nothing could ever persuade me to try that."

April 18, the four foreign commissioners who were to accompany Napoleon on his journey and be responsible for his safety, met at the Palace of Fontainebleau. They were the Russian General Shouvaloff, the Austrian General Roller, the English Colonel Campbell, and the Prussian General Turchsess. The 20th was fixed upon for the start.

Napoleon had not then begun to doubt Marie Louise, whom he regarded as a victim, not an accomplice of the Coalition. He knew that she had just seen her father at Rambouillet, and felt sure that she had expressed only the noblest feelings. He still hoped to see her soon, and so far from uttering any reproaches, he wrote to her affectionate letters like the following, which is without date, though presumably written April 19:—

My dear Louise: I have received your letter, and I learn all your sufferings, which add to my own. I am glad to hear that Corvisart encourages you; I "am most grateful to him; he confirms the good opinion I have always had of him; tell him so from me. Let him send me frequent word how you are. Try to go at once to Aix, as I hear Corvisart advises.

Keep well for—— and for your son, who needs your care. I am about starting for Elba, and will write to you from there. I shall make every preparation for receiving you. Write often; direct your letters to the Viceroy and to your uncle, if, as I hear, he has been made Grand Duke of Tuscany. Goodbye, my dear Louise Marie.

The very day he started from Fontainebleau for Elba, April 20, 1814, he wrote this letter to his wife: —

My Dear: I am leaving to rest tonight at Briare. Tomorrow morning I shall push on to Saint Tropez. Bausset, who will hand you this letter, will bring me news of you, and will tell you I am well. I hope that you will get better and be able to join me. Montesquiou, who left at 2 a.m., ought to be with you. I did not hear from you yesterday, but I hope that the Prefect of the Palace will join me this evening and will give me news of you. Goodbye, my dear Louise. You can always count on the courage, the calmness, and the friendship of your husband, Napoleon. A kiss to the little King.

These two letters make it clear he was still far from suspecting Marie Louise of ungrateful desertion. They show that when leaving Fontainebleau he still thought of his wife, whom then he had no reason for blaming; that he looked upon her as a model of gentleness and kindness, of religion and virtue, and that in good or evil fortune he was still proud of being her husband.

21

The Leave-Taking at Fontainebleau

History and legend mingle around Napoleon. Events of which people still living were eyewitnesses appear to us in such epic proportions, in such grandeur, that they seem to carry us back to distant ages. Napoleon has the air of a hero of antiquity, and the veterans of his Imperial Guard seem as remote as Cæsar's soldiers or the knights of Charlemagne. The leave-taking at Fontainebleau, the Courtyard of the White Horse, the Emperor, the grenadiers of the Old Guard, form a wonderful drama, set in a "wonderful stage, and with what brilliant characters! This dramatic scene was taken by Béranger for the subject of one of his most famous songs,—*Les Deux Grenadiers,*—which represents two soldiers talking together at the last midnight before Napoleon's departure.

In that sad night Napoleon was thinking of posterity, and he devised a way to lend a poetic interest to his departure for his parody of a kingdom at Elba, given him in exchange for the most magnificent empire in the world. And so well did he understand the art of striking the popular imagination, that this melancholy incident will, perhaps, make a deeper impression on future generations than all his triumphal entrances into the great capitals of Europe.

In the early morning of April 20, all the inhabitants of Fontainebleau had gathered to witness the memorable scene, crowding to the railing around the courtyard of the White Horse, where it was to take place. In this courtyard the Old Guard was drawn up. At noon the carriages had driven up to the foot of the Horseshoe Staircase, and General Bertrand had gone in to tell Napoleon that everything was ready. Napoleon came out of his room into the Gallery of Francis I.

There were assembled the few surviving relics of his once brilliant court,—the Duke of Bassano, General Belliard, Colonel de Bussè, Colonel Anatole de Montesquiou, Count Turenne, General Fouler, the Baron of Mesgrigny, Colonel Gourgaud, Baron Fain, Lieutenant-Colonel Athalin, Baron de la Place, Baron Leborgne d'Ideville, General Kosakovski, Colonel Vonsovitch. He replied to their tears by a grasp of the hand, a glance, and without saying a word, passed through the gallery and vestibule, and walked down the Horseshoe Staircase with a firm, swift step. As Lamartine says:

> The troops expressed a more solemn and religious feeling than cheers could express,—the honour, namely, of their fidelity, even in the darkest days, and the setting of the glory now about to sink behind the forest trees, behind the waves of the Mediterranean. They envied those of their companions to whom fortune had accorded exile in his island with their Emperor.

The Allies had permitted him to take with him but a single battalion, which was to be all he needed for conquering his throne. The men of the Old Guard had been asked how many would like to follow him, and all, without exception, offered themselves. Only four hundred were chosen. They were not in the courtyard, but were already on their way. Napoleon was at the foot of the staircase; the drums beat a salute. Why were they not draped in mourning? This was, in truth, the funeral of the Emperor, of the Empire, of the army. Their noise alone broke the silence. The soldiers were silent and gloomy. Napoleon made a sign that he wished to speak to them. The drums stopped beating; all seemed to hold their breath.

"Soldiers of the Old Guard," the Emperor began, "I say goodbye to you. For twenty years I have ever found you on the path to honour and to glory. In these last days, as in those of our prosperity, you have never ceased to be models of bravery and fidelity. With men like you our cause was not lost; but if it had no end, the war would have been a civil one, and France would have been only more unhappy. Hence I sacrificed my interests to those of my country, and I leave. Do you, my friends, continue to serve France. Its happiness will be my only thought— the sole object of my prayers. Do not mourn my lot. If I have consented to outlive myself, it is in order yet to serve your glory. I wish to record the great deeds we have done together."

Here Napoleon's voice broke. He gave way to his emotion for a moment, and then went on:

Goodbye, goodbye, my children. I should like to press you all to my heart. Let me at least kiss your flag!

At these words, General Petit, a man as modest as he was brave, seized the flag, and stepped forward. Napoleon embraced the general and kissed the eagle of the standard. Then nothing was to be heard for a few minutes but half-suppressed sobs, and the old grenadiers were seen wiping the tears from their weather-beaten faces. Napoleon, who was deeply affected, controlled himself by a mighty effort, raised his head, and in a firmer voice called out: "Goodbye, once more, goodbye, my old companions. Let this last kiss pass into your hearts!" Then he tore himself away from those about him, and covering his face with his hands, sprang into his carriage, which at once started on the first stage of his exile.

"What more shall I say? "asks General de Ségur, in his *Memoirs*. "The Grand Army, the Empire, the Emperor, all was over! The Genius that had supported me vanished with Napoleon. Now that I have come to this end of so much greatness, it seems to me that my literary life is over, as was our military career; that there was no more history

211

for the historian as there was no more war for warriors. It is a bitter and grievous memory that we recall of a country to be reconquered, of an affront to be avenged, of all the glory with which we were still defending ourselves, when suddenly our arms fell powerless to our side, and in the prime of life our disappointed hearts had to begin a new career in strange circumstances."

No scene has more deeply impressed the world than this leave-taking at Fontainebleau. No poet ever invented a more memorable incident. This extraordinary man, great in either event of fortune, knew how to touch even his enemies. The four foreign commissioners and their suite did not understand a word that the Emperor said, yet they could not conquer the emotion that seized them at the pathetic spectacle. Napoleon and his Old Guard have been sung in foreign lands as well as in France, by Lord Byron and by Heine.

Byron celebrates the 20th of April, 1814, in his poem, "To Napoleon":—

Must thou go, my glorious chief,
Sever'd from the faithful few?
Who can tell thy warrior's grief,
Maddening o'er that long adieu?

Woman's love and friendship's zeal,
Dear as both have been to me—
What are they to all I feel,
With a soldier's faith for thee?

Heine's poem, "The Two Grenadiers," is well known. It has been set to music by Schumann. A Bavarian dramatist has written a play, *Josephine Bonaparte,* which introduces the leave-taking at Fontainebleau. It has had great success at Munich, and when the actor who takes the part of Napoleon Bonaparte comes down the staircase and bids farewell to his old companions, the Germans are as much moved as the French.

22

The Journey to Elba

Napoleon's journey to Elba was full of incident, but it began calmly. General Drouot drove on ahead in one carriage; Napoleon followed in another with General Bertrand; then came the four commissioners of the Allied Powers. April 20, they stopped for the night at Briare; the 21st at Nevers; the 22nd at Roanne. The Emperor sent for the mayor of this town, and said to him:

> You ought to have here six thousand men of the army of Spain. If I had not been betrayed more than fourteen times a day, I should still be on the throne.

So far Napoleon encountered no hostile feeling on his way. Everywhere he stopped, he talked with the officials, and he had the consolation of hearing cries of "Long live the Emperor!" The first part of the way he had been escorted by detachments of cavalry,—a useless precaution, because in the Bourbonnais the attitude of the populace was friendly; but the escort was dismissed just when it would have been of service, and Napoleon was in as great peril of his life as if he had been on the battlefield. He passed through Lyons, April 23, at about eleven o'clock at night, without the knowledge of any one in the city. The 24th he reached Péage-de-Roussillon, a little village on the Rhone, and there he breakfasted.

As he was pushing on towards Valence, he met Marshal Augereau, Duke of Castiglione. "Where are you going like that?" he asked, grasping him by the arm; "Are you going to the court?"

Augereau answered that at that moment he was on his way to Lyons. This man of the 18th *Fructidor*, formerly a fanatical Republican, was hastening to join the Bourbons and to abjure the tricolour. April 16, from his headquarters at Valence, he had issued a proclamation to his soldiers, in which he said:

> Soldiers, you are freed from your oaths, by the nation, in which the sovereignty resides, and still more, if more were necessary, by the abdication of a man who, after immolating millions of victims to his cruel ambition, has not known how to die as a soldier. The nation summons Louis XVIII. to the throne. Born a Frenchman, he will be proud of your glory, and will gladly surround himself with your leaders; a descendant of Henri IV., he will have his heart; he will love the soldiers and the people.
>
> Let us then swear fidelity to Louis XVIII., and to the Constitution which presents him to us; let us raise the true French flag which abolishes every emblem of a revolution now ended, and soon you will find in the gratitude of your king and of your country a just reward for your noble deeds." The Emperor, doubtless still ignorant of this proclamation, talked for about a quarter of an hour with the hero of Castiglione, and kissed him on leaving. It has been said that an hour later he said to General Koller, the Austrian commissioner: "I have just heard of Augereau's infamous proclamation; if I had known about it when I met him, I should have combed his hair for him.

Napoleon passed through Valence, which had been one of his first garrisons when an obscure officer of artillery, but he did not stop there. The soldiers of Augereau's corps, though they all wore the white cockade, shouted, "Long live the Emperor!" But after Valence there were no more cheers; he encountered nothing but imprecations and curses.

As Napoleon was passing through Orange, April 25, he was greeted with cries of, "Long live the King! Long live Louis

XVIII.!" The same day, shortly before reaching Avignon, where he was to change horses, he encountered a number of men assembled, who shouted furiously: "Long live the King! Hurrah for the Allies! Down with the tyrant! the wretch! the beggar!"

A little further, at the village of Orgon, the popular fury was at its height. Before the inn where he was to stop there had been raised a gallows, on which swung a figure covered with blood, with an inscription on his breast: "This, sooner or later, will be the tyrant's lot!" The infuriated crowd climbed upon Napoleon's carriage, with the most savage insults. Count Shouvaloff, the Russian commissioner, had much difficulty in calming them.

An eye-witness, the Abbé Ferrucci, Cardinal Gabrielli's secretary, thus describes the terrible scene:

Orgon, April 25. A most noteworthy and unexpected incident took place today, in my presence. The ex-Emperor Napoleon was passing through *incognito,* with three carriages, at eight in the morning: the other carriages had .already gone through. The people, who spy out everything, gathered. Napoleon was to stop for breakfast, but he could not. All shouted: 'Death to the tyrant! Long live the King!' They burned him in effigy before his eyes, and held up before him figures stabbed and covered with blood.
Some climbed up on his carriage and shook their fists in his face, crying, 'Death to the tyrant!'
Some women, seizing stones, shouted, 'Give me back my son!' It was a painful spectacle, inconsistent with honour, humanity, and religion. For my part, I should have been glad to protect him with my own body.

The peril grew greater every moment. Napoleon had good reason to believe that his wonderful career was to come to a most terrible end. Sir Walter Scott, though generally most hostile to the Emperor, does not hesitate to say:

The danger was of a new and peculiarly horrible description, and calculated to appal many to whom the terrors of a field of battle were familiar. The bravest soldier might shudder at a death like that of the De Witts.

If we may believe the report of the Prussian commissioner, Count Von Waldburg Truchsess, the account of which Count Shouvaloff certified to Chateaubriand, the Emperor, when a quarter of a league from Orgon, thought it necessary to disguise himself; he put on a round hat with a white cockade, and got into a wretched blue overcoat; then he mounted a post-horse and galloped on ahead of his own carriage, in order to pass for a courier. The commissioners, who were not aware that he had changed, his dress, followed at some distance. Near Saint Canat, he entered a miserable inn, on the highroad, called *La Calade.*

"It was not till we were near Saint Canat," says the Prussian commissioner, "that we heard of the Emperor's disguise and of his arrival at this inn; he was accompanied by but a single courier; his whole suite, from the general to the scullion, wore white cockades, with which they seemed to have provided themselves beforehand. His valet came up to us, and begged us to make him pass for Colonel Campbell, the name he had given to the hostess when he arrived.

We promised to comply with this request, and I went first into a sort of chamber, where I was surprised to find the former monarch of the world buried in deep thought, with his head resting in his hands. I did not recognize him at first, and went nearer. He sprang up when he heard my steps, and I saw his face wet with tears. He made me a sign not to say anything, made me sit down by him, and all the time the hostess was in the room, talked to me about indifferent things.

We sat down at the table; but since the meal had not been prepared by his own cooks, he could not make up his mind to eat anything lest he should be poisoned. He talked a good deal, and was very pleasant. When we were alone, and our hostess, who waited on us, had gone away, he told us why he felt that his life was in danger; he was convinced that the French Government had taken measures to have him abducted or assassinated in this region. To convince us that his fears were well grounded, he told us of his talk with his hostess, who had not recognized him.

'Well,' she asked, 'have you met Bonaparte?'

' No,' he replied.

She went on, 'I wonder whether he will save himself; I always think the people are going to murder him, and I'm sure he will deserve it! Tell me, are they going to ship him to his island?'

'Oh, yes.'

'They'll drown him, won't they?'

'I hope so,' answered Napoleon. 'So you see to what danger I am exposed.'

This man in disguise, weeping in a miserable roadside inn, is he who was crowned Emperor of the French at Notre Dame, and King of Italy in the cathedral of Milan. This was the man of destiny, the new Caesar, the modern Charlemagne, who appeared at Dresden two years before as the King of Kings; to such strange misery had he fallen. Napoleon naturally dreaded dying there in this wretched hole, disguised as he was, and with the white cockade in his hat. Yet escape from his perils was not easy. Napoleon knew well these Southern people. Early in his career he had seen them at work, and they were as zealous now in their fervour for Royalism as they had been for the Republic: the White Terror promised to be as pitiless as the Red Terror had been.

Meanwhile, night had fallen, cold and dark, but on that account offering Napoleon a better protection than a strong escort. A violent mistral was raging, and this, with the darkness of the night, prevented the populace from gathering about this inn. Nevertheless, a good many suspected that the Emperor was there, and made their way thither. The foreign commissioners in vain tried to convince them that they were mistaken; that Napoleon was not there.

"We don't want to do him any harm," they said; "we only

want to look at him to see what effect misfortune has had upon him. We shall at the most only utter a few reproaches, and tell him the truth, which he has so seldom heard."

The commissioners succeeded in dissuading them and in calming them. Then someone appeared who promised to maintain order at Aix, if he could be given a letter for the mayor of that place. His offer was accepted, and the man started for Aix, returning soon with the assurance that the mayor had taken measures to prevent any disorder. It was midnight. The crowd that had assembled at the doors of the inn had for the most part dispersed; only a few were left, with lanterns. Napoleon decided to leave. But first he thought it prudent to put on a new disguise; hence, wishing to pass for a foreign officer, he put on General Roller's uniform, and wrapped himself up in General Shouval-off's cloak. Then, half an hour after midnight, they started out into the black and blustering night, eluding the few inquisitive men who still lingered about and turned the light of their dark-lanterns on the carriages.

When the Emperor tried to poison himself at Fontainebleau, could he have foreseen this deepest humiliation,— that he should wear a foreign uniform to escape being massacred by Frenchmen? Probably not; reality was to outdo his worst apprehensions. The Prussian commissioner, in his account, has no word of compassion for the defeated giant; he says:

> The Emperor did not regain confidence; he stayed in the Austrian general's carriage, and bade the coachman smoke,—a familiarity which would less betray his presence. He even asked General Roller to sing; and when he said he did not know how to sing, Bonaparte told him to whistle; and so he drove on, crouching in one of the corners of the carriage, pretending to sleep, lulled by the General's charming music, breathing the incense of the driver's pipe.

Chateaubriand exclaims that such a story is odious reading.

"What," he asks, "the commissioners could not give better

protection to the man for whom they had the honour of being responsible? Who were they, to put on such airs of superiority to a man like that? Bonaparte said with truth that he might have made the journey in the company of a part of his guard. They were plainly indifferent to his fate; they enjoyed his degradation; they gladly gave their consent to the marks of contempt which the victim required for his safety; it is pleasant to have under one's feet the destiny of the man who used to walk on the loftiest heads, and to avenge haughtiness by insult!

So the commissioners have no word, even of philosophic reflection, on such a change of fortune, to warn man of his nothingness and of the greatness of God's judgments! In the ranks of the Allies there had been many flatterers of Napoleon; when one has gone on his knees before force, he has no right to triumph in misfortune.

It is easy to understand the impression made on the Emperor's mind by his journey through Provence. It possibly explains his indulgence to the Imperialists who turned Royalists. He must have remembered that even he, the Emperor, had been forced to cry "Long live the King!" and to disguise, not merely his feelings, but also his person. He knew how rare was the stoicism of a Cato or a Brutus, and when he returned from Elba, he blamed no one of his ministers or marshals for turning their coats. He was past all possibility of surprise, and his extremes of good and evil fortune taught him at once compassion and contempt.

The end of the journey was without incident after leaving Aix. April 26, they breakfasted at Saint Maximin. Napoleon still wore General Koller's uniform. "You would not have recognized me in these clothes?" he asked of the sub-prefect of Aix; then he added, pointing to the commissioners:

These gentlemen induced me to put them on, deeming it necessary for my safety. I might have had an escort, but I refused, preferring to trust to French loyalty. I had no reason to regret this confidence from Fontainebleau to Avignon, but since then I have run much danger. The Provence people disgrace themselves.

Then he told them that when he was an artillery officer he had been sent into this country to set free two Royalists who were about to be hanged for wearing the white cockade. "It was only with great difficulty," he went on, "that I saved them from the "hands of those madmen, and now they are beginning the same excesses against those who refuse to put on the white cockade. Such is the inconsistency of the French."

In the evening of April 26 they reached the castle of Bouillidou, near Luc, where they found Princess Pauline Borghese, who was much moved when she saw her brother. There were Austrian troops nearby, charged with escorting the Emperor and seeing to his embarkment. Without further danger, he reached Fréjus, April 27, and thence he wrote to Corvisart:

> I have received your letter of the 22nd. I am glad to notice your good conduct when so many have conducted themselves ill. I am grateful to you, and it confirms the opinion I had already formed of your character. Give me news of Marie Louise, and never doubt my affection for you. Do not give way to melancholy thoughts; I hope that you will long be spared to do good and to make your friends happy.

The fifteenth article of the treaty of April 11, 1814, ran thus:

> The Imperial Guard will furnish a detachment of from twelve to fifteen hundred men, of all arms of the service, to serve as escort, to Saint Tropez, the place of sailing:

This article had not been carried out. Napoleon did not have the stipulated escort, and he did not sail from Saint Tropez. The sixteenth article was also unobserved; it said:

> There shall be supplied an armed corvette and the transports necessary to conduct to their destination His Majesty the Emperor and his household. The *corvette* shall remain His Majesty's property.

The French Government sent the brig, *Inconstant,* but Napoleon refused to sail in it.

"If the government," he said, "had known what was due to itself, it would have sent me a three-decker, and not an old worthless brig, which my dignity forbids me boarding."

The Emperor preferred to take the English frigate, *Undaunted,* which Colonel Campbell had had prepared.

April 27, Napoleon, who was to embark the next day in this frigate, in the gulf of Saint Raphael, invited to dinner, at Fréjus, the four foreign commissioners, Count Klamur, and the captain of the English ship.

"There he resumed all his Imperial dignity," says the Count of Waldburg. "He spoke to us with rare openness of his plans for the aggrandizement of France at our expense; he explained how he had meant to turn Hamburg into another Antwerp, and to make the harbour of Cuxhaven like that of Cherbourg. He pointed out to us what no one had noticed, that the Elbe was as deep as the Scheldt, and that a port could be built at its mouth like the one that made Belgium powerful. He spoke with such passion and vivacity of his fleets at Toulon, Brest, and Antwerp, of his Hamburg army, and of his mortars at Hyeres, with which he could throw shells three thousand paces, that one would have thought that all still belonged to him.

After dinner he took leave of the Russian and Prussian commissioners: only the English and Austrian commissioners were to accompany him to Elba. He took with him Generals Bertrand and Drouot, the Pole, Major Gerzmanofsky, two quartermasters of the palace, a paymaster, a physician, two secretaries, a house-steward, a valet, two cooks, and six servants. An escort of Austrian hussars accompanied him to the harbour of Saint Raphael, where he was received with military honours and a salute of twenty-four cannon. He set sail, April 28, at 9 p.m. May 3, he anchored in the roadstead of Porto Ferrajo, and on the 4th, he landed amid the cheers of the inhabitants, who were proud of their sovereign.

23

The Last Days of Marie Louise
in France

While Napoleon was thus on his way from Fontainebleau to Elba, what had become of the Empress, Marie Louise? We left her at Orleans, April 12, 1814, harassed and ill, weeping and wondering what was her duty. The same day, Baron de Bausset arrived, bringing her a letter from Napoleon and one from Metternich. The Austrian Minister assured Marie Louise that she should be free to lead an independent life, with the right of succession for her son, and he indicated that the best thing for her to do would be to go to Austria with her son to await her choice between the place where the Emperor Napoleon might be and her own establishment; he added that the Emperor Francis would have the happiness of helping to dry the tears which his unhappy daughter had only too many reasons for shedding; that she could be quiet for a season and free to decide upon the future, and that she might bring with her such persons as she best trusted.

Shortly after she received this letter, Prince Paul Esterhazy and Prince Wenezel-Lichtenstein reached Orléans with another letter from Metternich, telling her that the Duchies of Parma and Piacenza had been granted her, revertible to her son, and he asked her to go at once to the castle of Rambouillet to meet her father.

Marie Louise, who had long desired this interview, and was

very anxious to plead not only her own cause, but also that of her husband and son, readily agreed. She left Orléans, April 11, at 8 p.m., under the escort of some of the cavalry of the Imperial Guard. At Angerville, however, their place was taken by some Cossacks, who brandished their long pikes about the carriages as if they were a convoy of prisoners. In fact, from this moment Marie Louise was really a captive.

When, April 13, at noon, she reached Rambouillet, worn out with mental suffering and bodily fatigue, she found the roadway and the interior of the castle guarded by Russian troops. She regretted her haste in leaving Orleans, for she learned that her father would not be in Paris till the next day and would not come to Rambouillet till April 16.

The 12th, Marie Louise might have joined Napoleon at Fontainebleau; the 13th that was impossible. The foreigners, to whom she had imprudently entrusted herself, would not have permitted it. Up to that time, that is to say, up to April 13, Napoleon, as we have said, on account of his intention to kill himself, did not care to see again his wife and son. But as soon as he renounced his plan of suicide, he longed to press them to his heart.

The 13th, he sent General Cambronne to Orléans with two battalions of the Guard. Since he had heard that one of the reasons that prevented the Empress from going to Fontainebleau was the dread of being stopped on the way by the allied troops, he doubtless sent this escort to protect her. But General Cambronne arrived too late; Marie Louise was already on her way to Rambouillet.

The Empress spent the 13th, 14th, and 15th in feverish impatience to see her father. At one moment she was pacing her apartment in great agitation; the next she was motionless, shedding torrents of tears. The visit that Queen Hortense made brought her no consolation; she saw that Josephine's daughter suspected her of desiring to leave Napoleon.

In the afternoon of April 16, a very plain open carriage brought to Rambouillet the Emperor of Austria, accompanied only by Prince Metternich. Marie Louise, followed by her son and Madame de Montesquiou, went down to the foot of the palace staircase. When she saw her father, she burst into tears, and even before she kissed him, she placed the King of Rome in his arms. This was a silent reproach which the Emperor of Austria must well have understood when for the first time he pressed to his heart the grandson whom he had never seen, and now beheld in circumstances so agonizing for the unhappy mother.

Marie Louise barely took time to present to her father such members of her household as happened to be present, and hastened with him into her room.

Her father was no less moved than she was. The little boy, whose fate was already so pathetic, won his admiration; he gazed at him tenderly, and promised to look after him, as if to atone for not having defended him more warmly. Henceforth, Marie Louise and the King of Rome lived only under the protection of Austria. Two battalions of Austrian infantry and two squadrons of Austrian cavalry took the place of the Russian troops on guard at Rambouillet.

The Emperor Francis spent the night there, and left the next morning at nine, having persuaded his daughter to go to Vienna. He took good care not to tell her that he condemned her never to see her husband again, and he led her to suppose that after she had rested awhile in the bosom of her family, she should be free to divide her time between the Duchy of Parma and the island of Elba. But these promises did not satisfy Marie Louise. Her interview with her father, so far from allaying her anxiety, only redoubled it. With her elbows on her knees, and her head in her hands, she meditated and wept.

April 19, Marie Louise received at Rambouillet a visit which was extremely painful to her, but her father insisted on it, namely, from the Emperor Alexander. As the Duke of Rovigo says in his *Memoirs*:

The Czar must have seen from her face, which had been bathed with tears for twenty days, what effect he produced on her. Doubtless he did not know that the Empress had been informed in detail of everything that had taken place in Paris before and during his reception of the deputation of marshals. But she knew all the plans framed against her husband, and she would have had to possess great self-control to keep her face calm before the instigator of the griefs by which she was tormented.

Alexander apologized for the liberty he took in presenting himself before the Empress without first securing her permission. He added that he came with the consent of the. Emperor of Austria, and warmly assured her of his sympathy and devotion.

"He was so amiable, so easy," says the Baron de Bausset, "that we were almost tempted to believe that nothing serious had happened in Paris. After breakfast he asked the Empress if he might see her son. Then turning towards me,—for I had the honour of meeting him at the Erfurt Congress,—he asked me if I would kindly take him to 'the little King': those are his own words. I preceded him, after sending word to Madame de Montesquiou. When he saw the boy, the Emperor kissed him, played with him, and looked at him attentively."

Marie Louise treated the Czar politely, but coldly.

As soon as he heard that the Empress was at Rambouillet, Napoleon gave up all thought of asking her to join him. He knew that there the Emperor of Austria would not let her come to him, and that Marie Louise was no longer free. Nevertheless, April 19, the day before he left Fontainebleau, he dictated to Baron Fain a letter for the Baron de Méneval, in which he. said:

Inasmuch as the Empress has made many inquiries of M. de La Place about the island of Elba, I send you the report of an officer of engineers who has just come from there: it is fuller than anything we have. You may show it to the Empress, if you think it will interest her.

Those last words are not without sadness,—"if you think it

will interest her." It seems as if he foresaw that desertion which throws such a cloud on the fame of Marie Louise.

The letter closed thus:

The Emperor was not able to leave today, because the preparations could not be completed; he will leave tomorrow, to pass through Nevers, Moulins, Lyons, Avignon, Aix, to Saint Tropez. Letters must be directed to Leghorn and Genoa, to the care of the Viceroy and of the King of Naples.

That same evening, April 19, there came another letter from Fontainebleau:

The Emperor starts at 9 a.m. tomorrow. He wrote to you this morning the road he means to take to Lyons through the Bourbonnais, to Saint Tropez, through Avignon and Aix. The Emperor would like to receive news from the Empress tomorrow evening at Briare, where he means to pass the night; he hopes also to find letters at Saint Tropez. In a word, His Majesty begs of you to write to him at every opportunity.

April 22, Marie Louise received at Rambouillet another visit even more disagreeable than that of the Emperor Alexander; that, namely, of the King of Prussia. After spending an hour with the Empress, this monarch asked the Baron de Bausset, as the Czar had done, to take him to "the little King." The King was less affectionate, less demonstrative, than the Emperor Alexander; but, like him, he kissed "the little King."

The same day the Austrian general, Count Kinski, accompanied by several officers, arrived at Rambouillet. He was to accompany Marie Louise to Vienna, and came to see about the preparations for the journey.

Marie Louise started from Rambouillet April 23, stopping a day at Grosbois, the castle of Berthier, Prince of Wagram, where she saw her father, who left on the 25th to dine in Paris with the Count d'Artois. Then she pushed on with her son, not stopping again. The Empress was accompanied by the Duchess of Montebello, the Countess of Brignoli, General Caffarelli, MM. de Saint Aignan, de Bausset, and de Méneval; the King of Rome by his governess, the Countess of Montesquiou, and by Madame Soufflot. The Duke of Rovigo says:

"She travelled under the escort of her father's troops, and took the road by which the Allies had marched from Basle to Paris. She passed through the departments of a country which, four years before, had raised triumphal arches to greet her, had scattered, flowers before her feet: It saw her leave as the last victim of the enemies who had ravaged its cities, and carrying with her the tie which, shortly before, had seemed to unite her more firmly with the French. Her heart was rent with anguish in this sad journey: everything was full of bitterness. She carried with her the regrets of all who had enjoyed the happiness of approaching her, and left behind her the memory of her virtues."

The Empress spent the night of April 25 at Provins, whence she wrote to Napoleon. The country presented a most doleful appearance: the ravages of war had left hideous traces. The harvests had been trampled beneath the feet of cavalry horses; everywhere were to be seen houses destroyed, villages in ashes.

The night of the 26th, she stopped at Troyes, in the house of M. de Mesgrigny, father of one of the Emperor's equerries; the 27th, at Châtillon, famous for its fruitless congress. The 28th, she reached Dijon, where the Austrian troops were drawn up to receive her as their Emperor's daughter. They had. wanted to welcome her with a salute and to illuminate the city, but she declined. That night she slept at Dijon; the next at Gray; the 30th at Vesoul; May 1st at Belfort; and May 2nd, she crossed the Rhine between Huningue and Basle, leaving French soil.

Marie Louise had spent but four years in France, and they had left a more painful than happy memory. Her happiness had not lasted more than two years, but had been darkened by many a cloud. The days of her prosperity came to an end with the Dresden interview. The Russian campaign was the beginning of a series of anxieties which ended in complete misery.

When Marie Louise recalled her eventful career, those four perturbed years must have seemed like a distressing nightmare. Her elevation and her fall were equally astounding. A single consolation was left ,her,—the thought that she had done her duty. In 1814 she could make herself no serious reproach. A good wife, a good mother, a good Regent, she had always obeyed Napoleon's orders, and he never once complained of her. All parties respected her and amid all the insults poured out on .her husband, no voice was raised to denounce or even to criticise her.

In their *Memoirs* the most ardent partisans of the Emperor, Méneval, Bausset, Savary, have only most flattering words for her. No Legitimist, no Republican, has attacked her. When she left France, everyone paid homage to her virtue and her character. Everyone felt sure that she would go to join her husband at Elba. She thought so herself; she had not yet felt the influence of the Count of Neipperg. The bonds uniting her to Napoleon were stretched, but not yet broken, and at first after her return in Germany, she had not ceased to be a Frenchwoman.

Time was needed to turn the dethroned Empress into an Austrian princess; the transformation only took place gradually. Drawn in opposite directions, the prey of contradictory influences, hesitating between two countries, as between her father and her husband, she at first experienced painful scruples and doubts. It was a difficult position for a young woman of twenty-two. Ambushes beset this victim of politics on all sides, and all possible plans were devised to prevent her going to Elba, whither her duty called her. Accustomed from infancy, as daughter and subject, to follow her father's wishes, she at last blindly accepted a yoke which relieved her of many responsibilities.

Being of a passive, submissive nature, she entrusted herself and her son to her father's care: it is he rather than she who deserves the blame of posterity. In any other time, she would have been a faithful wife, an excellent mother, an honoured sovereign, but she had not enough energy to play a proper part in such troublous days. For four years she had been a true Frenchwoman; but when she had returned to Germany, all the ideas, the prejudices, the passions of her girlhood reappeared, and she forgot her second county in her attachment for the land of her birth.

Thus happened to her what often happens to women who marry foreigners: they do not really change their nationality, but remain devoted daughters of their native land. Social conventions, even religious ties, are often powerless to destroy the work of nature, and marriage, sacred as it is, cannot uproot the memory of one's country. The Archduchess of Austria, the Duchess of Parma, Piacenza, and Guastalla succeeded to the Empress of the French, the Queen of Italy.

As for her son, not only did he cease to be the King of Rome, the Prince Imperial of France, he never was even Hereditary Prince of Parma. He was never to obtain the promised right of succession. The time was drawing near when he was to be robbed of the name of Bonaparte, the name of Napoleon, and was to be known only as Francis, Duke of Reichstadt.